English Girl, Girl,

German Boy

WORLD WAR II FROM BOTH SIDES ■

By
Tessa and Martin
Börner

Library and Archives Canada Cataloguing in Publication

Borner, Tessa
English girl, German boy : World War II from both sides /
Tessa and Martin Borner.

ISBN 0-9738926-0-9

1. Borner, Tessa. 2. Borner, Martin, 1929-.
3. World War, 1939-1945--Personal narratives, English.
4. World War, 1939-1945- Personal narratives, German. I. Borner,
Martin, 1929-   II. Title.

D811.5.B67 2005   940.54'8141   C2005-905012-8

Production and Design
Silvio Mattacchione and Co. / Studio Graziano and Associates Inc.
1251 Scugog Line 8, RR#1.
Port Perry, ON, Canada L9L 1B2
Telephone: 905.985.3555
Fax: 905.985.4005
silvio@silvio-co.com
graziano@lincsat.com

www.silvio-co.com

Printed in Canada by Friesens

Dedication

This book is dedicated

to the children of war everywhere,

and most of all to our children

and grandchildren.

We especially remember

our parents

who sacrificed so much

so that we could

live in peace.

About the Authors

Tessa and Martin were married in Canada in 1957 and are the parents of five children and the grandparents of eleven grandchildren. They now live in Costa Rica where they have owned a country bed and breakfast, *Posada Mimosa*, since 1994. They have welcomed thousands of guests from around the world.

Tessa is also the author of *Potholes to Paradise* which tells about their experiences living in Costa Rica.

Tessa and Martin

Web site http://www.mimosa.co.cr

Acknowledgements

First of all, we thank our granddaughter, Emilie Leonard, for suggesting the title for our book and for her continuing interest in our story. We also thank our children and grandchildren who have all urged us to write this book.

Tessa's mother's letters and notes have been invaluable, as well as the recorded interviews made with her by our daughter Megan. The memories of our son Jason and daughters Heidi, Megan, and Hilary give an excellent picture of life in East Germany during the Communist era.

We also thank Martin's parents for their letters describing life in Communist East Germany.

Thanks to Petra Dolle of the Dresden archives for giving us permission to print photos of Dresden. Our special thanks to our editor, Janice Dyer, who has done a wonderful job pulling the book together with her fine editing skills.

Table of Contents

Foreword

This book is about a very important time in history: before, during, and after World War II. The war began when Tessa was five years old and living in England and Martin was a ten-year-old boy living outside Dresden, Germany. We have used letters and recorded tapes from Tessa's mother to help describe life in Wales in the early 1900s and in Britain during and after World War II. In addition, Martin's father left a legacy of letters compiled during the Communist era (1945–1989) in the former East Germany. Through Martin's eyes, we learn how ordinary Germans suffered and how few first-hand accounts there are of the German story. For the sake of our children and grandchildren, we decided to write this book from "both sides of the war." As well, we hope to bring our message to others who may have only heard a one-sided story presented by the media.

Today, we see countless wars all over the world, mind-numbing slaughters played out on nightly television for the whole world to see, and we seem to have learned nothing from the past. Adolf Hitler was a madman, but there have been many others who have continued his evil practices right up until the present day. Genocide after genocide has been committed with the full knowledge of the world community, with little done to stop them.

English Girl,

German Boy

For over half a century, Germans have paid the price of Hitler's brief twelve year rule. Sixty years later, groups are still demanding money as retribution. The German nation has endured a collective guilt complex for far too long. Today's generation is still bombarded with anti-German propaganda and is blamed for the Nazi past when, for them, it is history. It is as though all Germans of Martin's generation are unjustly presumed to have been members of the Nazi party.

The question is, what nation is guilt-free? England certainly has its fair share of atrocities committed in the name of empire-building and colonial exploitation. How about the United States with its history of slavery and racial strife, or Israel with its domination of the Palestinians? Or the bombing of thousands of civilians in the Iraq War by the only nation who ever used "weapons of mass destruction" when it dropped atom bombs on Hiroshima and Nagasaki?

As children of both sides of WWII, we hope to contribute our story to the historical understanding of future generations. We won no medals, we stormed no beaches, we were not heroes. We were simply children caught up in a nightmare not of our making, guilty of nothing.

This book is dedicated to children of war everywhere, and most of all to our children and grandchildren.

Part One-English Girl
Tessa's Story

Tessa & Angela
in Bristol, circa 1938

Chapter One

My Mother, Peggy

Peggy and her family circa 1913. Her mother is seated with Peggy on her knee, her father is standing with eldest sister Elizabeth (Bessie) and eldest brother David who died in a mining accident. Standing in front on the left is Herbert, and Peggy's favourite brother Clifford is on the right. A sixth child, Sidney, was not yet born.

My mother was born Ellen Margaret Davies on October 7, 1909 in the small coal mining town of Mountain Ash, Glamorgan, South Wales. She was known as Peggy all her life. Her parents were Francis Davies born September 3, 1872 in Mountain Ash, and Ellen Williams born March 24, 1877 in Angle, Pembrokeshire, Wales. Peggy was the second youngest of their six children, and she took after her father as the only dark-haired child. The others all inherited beautiful red gold hair the colour of a gold coin and vivid blue eyes from Ellen.

Peggy's paternal grandmother was Elizabeth Picton, born in 1839 in Martletwy, Pembrokeshire. Family legend says there is a possible connection to Sir Thomas Picton, a famous Welsh general during the war with France, and also to Picton Castle. Most researchers think all the Pictons are linked since they descended from two Norman knights, brothers William and Philip de Picton, the original owners of

Picton Castle. They came from Normandy with William the Conqueror in 1066 and tried to conquer the Welsh but were unsuccessful. The Picton name is not a common one and is mostly found in Pembrokeshire, Wales, although there are towns in Canada, Australia, and New Zealand which bear the Picton name.

Ellen Williams had a Canadian connection through her half-brother Harry Williams who emigrated to Canada around 1871 and settled in Cornwall, Ontario. His brother Thomas left for Canada later. Harry and Thomas prospered in the new world working in real estate and the hotel business. Harry was said to have been mayor of Cornwall and the builder of the Cornwallis Hotel. Thomas had a son Evan Thomas who died September 7, 1958 without issue and left an inheritance of $55,161 to my grandmother. He also left properties at 130 Third St. West and 241–243–245 York St., Cornwall.

Francis and Ellen Davies brought up their family in Mountain Ash. It was not a pretty place. Mines scarred the beautiful Welsh valley, slag heaps dotted the landscape, and coal dust was everywhere. Most of the people worked in the mines—it was a tough life. Coal was used as fuel in fireplaces to heat houses and cook meals, and to fuel steam engines. It was an important commodity before electricity and gas.

Although my grandfather—known as Dad Dad to his grandchildren—worked as a coal hewer, he had other interests. He should have been a doctor, but the family could not afford to pay for his education. Instead, he was head of St. John Ambulance Brigade for the whole Aberdare valley, and joined the Royal Army Medical Corps during World War I. However, his greatest achievement was becoming a noted herbalist who

English Girl, German Boy

healed and treated local people. He had an herb garden and books of remedies and recipes which, for some reason, were destroyed by my grandmother, known as Mam Mam to her grandchildren. He was an avid gardener and my strongest memories are of him working in his garden, tending his vegetables and flowers. He insisted on a good education for all of his children, and they all went on to become successful people. He was especially proud of my mother who was the first woman in her town to go to college and who became a pharmacist. As we shall see, his insistence that she have a good livelihood served her well later on.

Peggy's Earliest Memories

Two of my mother's earliest memories were the deaths of two of her brothers. She was five when her oldest brother David was killed when he fell down a mine shaft. She remembered opening the door to find Mr. Mildon, the police, with a very white face and no smile, which was unusual for him. Suddenly, the house was full of people and her mother was crying. It was hard to believe that her 16-year-old brother had been killed—he just was not home any more. She always remembered the terrible sadness that filled the house. Peggy's father impressed upon her the explanation that David was gone because he had disobeyed the rule that they were not to play near the pit shaft at the colliery, and he had fallen down the pit shaft. That explanation stayed with her all her life.

During the First World War, Peggy's father served in a hospital in Weymouth for four years. Sidney was born in 1916 when my mother was seven and was their "war baby." The hospital was called Sidney Hall, and that is where her brother got his name. When Peggy was nine, Sidney was diagnosed with tuberculosis and was immediately quarantined, the main method of controlling outbreaks of communicable diseases. Sidney was only two when he was sent off to a sanitarium over the mountain from where they lived. After a few months, he was cured and was ready to come home. My grandmother was on her way to pick him up when news came that he had fallen out of his crib and had died.

In those days, if somebody had measles or chicken pox, by law a card had to be placed in the window and nobody was allowed into the house. When scarlet fever hit their house, a red card was put in the window. The bedroom door was open, but the doorway was completely covered by a white sheet soaked in carbolic acid to prevent the spread of germs. People died of these diseases because there were no vaccinations (except for smallpox) or antibiotics.

Daily Life—Early 1900s

When my mother was three, her father left for Australia, waving to them as he walked backwards down the path. He wanted to emigrate because conditions in Wales were very bad. My grandfather came back from Australia in 1913, after six months. It took him six weeks to go and six weeks to return, and he was seasick all the way. He went by boat because there were no commercial airliners at that time. He decided against Australia because of the heat: my grandmother had had sunstroke and would not have been able to stand it.

There were good reasons for leaving Wales in 1912. Colliers were only paid a shilling a day, and there was great unrest in the country. The English came in as landowners because there was so much coal in the ground. Lord Duffryn was the owner of all the land and the town had a very large cemetery called *mycererian*, which means field of gold. Lord Aberdare had charged the town for this piece of land for a cemetery. Lord Duffryn had bought up all the land and there was fighting because the English wanted the Welsh out. To defend Wales against England and other invaders (including the Romans), many castles were built early in its history and so Wales was never occupied by a foreign power.

Apart from the tragic deaths of her two brothers, my mother's childhood was a happy one. Saturdays and Sundays were important in my mother's memories, perhaps because the whole family—a sister, four brothers, and parents—was together. She especially looked forward to Saturdays when, in the morning, she would run to the stables where Jim, the Co-op store cart-horse, waited for her to curry him. He had to look his best to deliver the groceries to the many rows of houses. The doctor also made his house calls using a horse and trap. For Sunday school outings to the seaside, they used the charabanc which seated about 30 children and a few adults. There were no buses and certainly no school buses. The children walked three miles up the hills and three miles down to and from school—it was "shank's pony" everywhere (meaning travelling by foot).

The horse was Peggy's only distraction for a couple of hours, and then it was home to clean the cutlery. She cleaned the steel knives with powdered brick and the forks and spoons with Brasso while Peggy's Mam (mother) baked bread; the slap of the dough being kneaded was like music to her ears. Peggy's brothers split blocks of wood to make kindling for the coal fire which was the only source of heat in their stone house with flagstone floors. It was also used for all of their cooking. All of Saturday morning was taken up with my grandmother baking bread, fruit pies, currant cake, and little Welsh cakes to last for the week. The Welsh cakes were baked over the fire on a bake-stone, a one inch thick round of iron balanced over the fire by each hob created by the oven top and the hot water tank each side of the five bar deep grate. The toaster was hooked on the front of these bars, very similar to the present day barbecue holder for turning food during cooking.

The fireplace was a thing of beauty. My grand-mother black-leaded it every morning so that you could see your face in it, and the steel fender and fire irons shone like silver. The mantelpiece was edged with dark green plush twelve inches deep with a ball fringe. Sitting on the mantelpiece were twelve brass candlesticks shin-ing bright, six on each side, centred with a clock, moon and flowers painted on its face behind the glass door where a brass pendulum tick-tocked the hours away. Every fifteen minutes the clock chimed the passing of time, imitating the tone of Big Ben, that mighty clock in London. On the hour, it chimed twelve times. The clock fascinated Peggy, and she remembered wondering why it was always fussing to tell the time. It seemed to be the only disturbing element in her daily life.

One of my mother's daily joys was to watch her mother dress her hair. It was a source of wonder to see the waist-length golden hair tossed forward, her mother bending from the waist to vigorously brush the hundred strokes. Still bending forward, her mother then gathered the hair in one hand and twisted it into a rope-like skein. Upright, she wound the hair into a coil on top of her head. Hairpins kept the coil in place. With a final pat and tendrils pulled here and there, she was ready to face the day. The "hair tidy" waited on her dressing table to receive the combings from the brush. During Victorian times, most women had a hair tidy on their dressing table. It came in many styles: knitted, cro-cheted, or hand-painted china. My grandmother's was a

English
Girl,

German
Boy

hand-painted shallow round dish with a cover fashioned with a hole large enough to receive hair combings. These combings were later made into rolls known as "rats" which were added under the lady's hair, thus adding volume to the then fashionable hair style, the high pompadour.

As she grew older, my mother's home duties increased. My grandmother washed the dishes in a big enamel bowl on the kitchen table while Peggy dried them, then arranged them in "The Basket," a big, round cane basket. The cups were placed one inside the other making a snakelike circle and the saucers stood around the sides making what looked like a frill. Plates went behind the saucers, and in the middle stood the milk jug holding the spoons. Peggy's big brother, without ever having to be asked, staggered with The Basket to the pantry and deposited it on "The Stone," a wide shelf of slate where the butter, earthenware bread pan, milk, and cheese sat to keep cool. A side of bacon always hung in the pantry. Peggy was fascinated watching her mother slice off rashers, always the right thickness with the rind on. How lovely it was to pull the last bit of bacon off the rind through clenched teeth! Bacon fat was poured into a jam jar and slathered on fried bread to eat with the Sunday breakfast treat of salt-fish.

Peggy never heard her mother wondering what they would eat. She knew: joint on Sunday, cold on Monday the devil's birthday (so-called because it was washday), shepherd's pie on Tuesday, liver on Wednesday, stew on Thursday, fish on Friday, and Saturday was heavenly fish and chips from Marshall's the fish shop. Peggy and her brother took a large tureen and put in the order of ten cutlets of cod or haddock and a shillings worth of chips and paid two shillings and sixpence for the lot. They covered the tureen with a cloth and, on their way home, lifted it to snitch a chip or two, and then walked with their mouths open so Mam would not detect their sin! Thick rounds of home-made bread and butter completed the meal.

On Sundays, everybody went off to chapel in their Sunday best. Peggy's father wore his blue serge suit and stiff white collar to which was attached a white dickey so his Welsh flannel undershirt could not be seen. Before leaving for chapel at eleven o'clock, the "joint" was put in the oven, which was part of the magnificent fireplace. Beef, pork, lamb, veal: in that order all through the year each Sunday. After chapel, the family walked home to be greeted with the glorious aroma. They always ate dinner around two o'clock.

All was quiet in the house after Sunday dinner. Mam and Dad took a nap while Peggy and her siblings went to Sunday school. Her teacher was Mr. Harris, the bank, so called because he was the manager of the local bank. It identified him from the other Mr. Harris, the ironmonger, and Mr. Harris, the blacksmith. Peggy then walked home again to find tea ready, including the cake she had made in all its glory, tinned fruit and custard, bread and butter, and tea, of course. Then it was chapel again at six o'clock, after which everyone strolled around the Duffryn Woods, stopping to talk with friends.

Peggy's parents were staunch Baptists so they were forbidden to play cards and sing popular songs on Sunday, and there was certainly no alcohol in their house. Peggy never did become a Baptist. At the age of 16 when they were received into the faith to become a member of the Chapel, she refused. Her parents respected her reasons, that she could see no wrong in playing cards, etc., since the majority of her friends and their families did not seem to be possessed by the devil. Peggy later became a Roman Catholic after the death of her first husband, and that faith greatly sustained her throughout her life.

Winter time, aunts, uncles, and cousins came to the house after chapel. Aunt Martha always turned back her long, black skirt so the fire would not turn it green. For some reason, Peggy's mother always kept her hat on during these visits. Was it to show off her lovely hats? They all were beautiful. One Peggy especially remembered was shiny, blue straw with purple grapes covered with grey chiffon. After tea and cake, they all sang hymns around the piano. Peggy's oldest brother tried to play his bugle quietly, her brother Clifford played the flute, and her sister Bess played the Welsh harp.

Peggy learned by doing. Her mother baked, so she baked. Her mother sewed, so she sewed. Her mother knitted, so did she. Peggy also learned the art of gardening from her parents, who were superb gardeners. She learned to cut back plants that they transplanted so the strength went to the roots. Bushes were pruned for the winter so ice and snow would not break the branches. Bulbs were planted before the snow came, and the beds cleaned so they would not harbour bugs for the winter. Peggy secretly thanked her father for the joy and knowledge he passed on. It was a wonderful inheritance from her parents. Peggy's younger brother's garden won the championship cup five years in succession for the best garden in Northamptonshire, England. Her oldest brother in Leicester and his son also won awards, as did her nephew Peter Cole who was a steady winner at flower shows and had a room full of trophies and medals for both flowers and vegetables. Many years later and far from Wales, Peggy and her husband created a rock garden on the Island of Orleans, Quebec which was visited by people from all over the world. Today Peggy's daughters and grandchildren carry on the tradition with gardens of their own.

During her growing years, Peggy was encouraged to read with her family before going to bed. Her parents chose the reading material and Peggy and her two brothers read the marked paragraphs aloud. They enjoyed the neighbourhood games of "Weak Horses and Strange Donkeys," hopscotch, hide and seek, marbles, skipping to songs, hand-ball, football, cat and doggie, rounders, and many more games. Evenings, the family played cards, dominoes, and checkers. Peggy belonged to the Brownies, Girl Guides, sang in her hometown's girl's choir, and each year competed at *Eisteddfods* (festivals of music). At school, apart from the normal curriculum, she learned to dance and was in the drama class. She also joined the local drama society, and time was taken up in rehearsals and increasing her circle of friends.

At Christmas time, Peggy and her family made their own decorations, and the gifts were also handmade; one gift for the whole family was usually a new game they could all enjoy. They exchanged visits with friends and relations, always keeping in close touch with family. Birthdays were important occasions; having a special friend join the family for a meal was a great treat.

Politics were very different in those times. Members of parliament were honorary members and so were not paid. Each little town had a representative, and Peggy's town's representative was George Hall. She remembered a song all the children sang: "Vote, vote, vote for Georgie Hall, push old Stanton up a tree, Georgie is the man and we'll have him if we can, so vote, vote, vote, for Georgie Hall!" Nobody would ever dare ask another person who they were voting for—it just was not done!

Shopping in Wales was a social event. It took a whole morning's walk to get the necessary items for a meal. They stopped at Evans the Butcher for meat, Williams the Dairy for milk, butter, and eggs, Longs the Grocer for dry goods, Collins the Fresh Fish for fish, Pugh the Draper for fabrics, and Jones the Chemist for medicine. They bought vegetables and fruit at the green-grocer. They gathered all the news on the trek, and it gave the dog a good walk. This ritual took place every day because refrigerators were unheard of. Peggy was fascinated by the variety of shopping bags people carried. Some had baskets, while others had string bags so you did not have to guess what the Roberts' were having for dinner! Prams (baby carriages) were a prime means of transportation. Sometimes the baby could hardly be seen for all the brown paper bags stuffed with groceries! Mam had a pretty, sturdy brown cane basket with flowers on it, and she always carried a worn black leather purse.

If you were short of money while shopping, the amount was written on a slate with chalk: you were buying "on tick." When you paid, a tick was put along-side your purchase. The Co-op was the forerunner of the charge account of today. One had to buy so many shares to belong, and all bought items were put in an exercise book. The Co-op sold everything, similar to today's department store. It was smart to pay for all you bought because then you received a dividend, but peo-ple could carry over what they could not manage to pay. This was a boon when the man of the house was laid off from the coal mine due to sickness, injury, or strikes.

Everybody paraded "the Mount," the name of the main street in the town, on Saturday night. There were canvas canopied stalls selling every kind of sweets.

Peggy and her family's favourite treat was lady fingers, pink and white striped peppermint flavoured sweets, enough to last a week. Gas jets lit the stalls because there was no electricity in the town, and lamp posts were also lit with gas, a step up from oil lamps.

Summer Holidays

The annual family holiday, the month of August, was spent at the seaside. My mother remembered the anticipation she felt when they went to Weymouth in the south of England. It was a most exciting experience, each member of the family packing his or her own suitcase. When the day arrived, they went to their bedrooms at Mam's command, "time to pack," no second urging necessary. Now the baby of the family (6 years old), Mam helped Peggy to pack the "proper" way.

Arriving at the station in Jones, the milk's cart, they eagerly awaited the arrival of the train which would take them to paradise—Weymouth! Peggy clutched her Mam's hand and had to stand back from the edge of the platform so the train would not suck her in as it fussed and steamed into position. It was always a game to try to be standing right opposite a door as the train stopped. It was her big brother's job to open the door with the magnificent shining handle and to help Mam in. There were glorious red plush seats on each side of the compartment and it was a scramble for the window seats. Mam would console whoever was last by declaring that everybody would have a turn by the window. Peggy's father heaved the suitcases up on the rack which looked like a hammock stretched on iron frames.

The journey took about four hours, and the changing countryside always fascinated them: green fields with sheep grazing and trees so shining green, they somehow seemed so different from the ones at

English
Girl,

German
Boy

home. Peggy later learned the coal dust of their valley covered their trees, turning them dull. When they passed out of Wales into England, they opened their lunch basket and attacked with great gusto. Then came the excitement of being the first to see the white horse on the hills of Westbury. The hills were limestone, and they never found out who carved the image of a prancing horse, a signal they would arrive in Weymouth in half an hour. It was a joy to see Mr. Toby waiting with dear Dobbin and the shining trap. It was always Peggy's privilege to sit up with Mr. Toby and hold the reins with him. His black, shining top hat always fascinated her. Dobbin's patient clip clop was so restful and a contrast to the rush and noise of traffic today.

"Elsie dear," Toby's wife, greeted them heartily and always smelled of apple pie. For many years, Peggy really thought her name was "Elsie dear" because Mr. Toby never called her by any other name. Peggy and her siblings gathered limpets off the rocks and cooked them in Elsie dear's kitchen. The beach was wonderful. They swam and built sand castles, and Peggy's brothers built amazing forts. There were no boats, canoes, or frisbees and they never seemed to spend money on anything. Deck chairs cost three pennies for a half day, but they were only for Peggy's parents. They looked forward to strawberries and cream afternoon tea and a visit to the Wishing Well where they solemnly threw in a penny and made a wish, fully convinced it would come true. They listened to concerts in the bandstand on the promenade in the evenings. The blissful time came to an end all too soon and it was time to leave. The family repeated their annual visit to Weymouth until 1926, the year of the terrible General Strike.

Education

Before going to Central school, Peggy attended Standard school where she had an excellent general education in all subjects. Character-building was also stressed, along with manners, deportment, elocution, and drama lessons. There was great emphasis on language and grammar, and it is where she learned English. Peggy only spoke Welsh until the age of 10. As the children learned English, speaking Welsh in their family gradually petered out. At home, her mother firmly insisted on politeness, good table manners, and respect for others. Peggy's brothers always had to stand up when grownups entered a room.

Peggy's father was a strict, stern man who gave his children many lessons on building their characters. Peggy vividly remembered one Saturday night when her father decided they should have an insight into the "sins of iniquity," the chief sin being the abuse of alcohol, according to him. She was wrapped in a warm coat and muffler, and off she went with her brothers and parents "down the Mount," the main street. The pubs were the busiest places and the main source of entertainment. They watched drunken husky Irishmen and, to their shame, Welshmen too, being frog-marched through the streets to the police station and locked up for the night. Frog marching meant that policemen clutched each arm and each leg and carried the culprit face down, promptly lowering him to the ground and bouncing if he protested. Judging from the howls of agony coming from the culprits, it must have been painful treatment. Watching this treatment was meant to convey to the children the wages of the sin of imbibing too much alcohol.

My mother graduated from the Central school when she was only 15 and knew then that she wanted to be a pharmacist, or chemist as it is known in Britain. Her schooling was in Welsh and English, but later she had to drop Welsh and take Latin to study pharmacy. She also majored in science and chemistry. Peggy was too young to be accepted into college, so she went to work for Mr. Rees, the chemist, and a good friend of the family. By doing this, she got her practical experience first before going to college. Peggy enjoyed her time working, getting to know all the people. It was a wonderful time in her life and she belonged to the tennis club and the hockey club, rode Welsh ponies, and enjoyed an active social life.

Great Strike—1926

Around 500 B.C. the Celts migrated from Northern Europe to Britain and started hill settlements in Wales. They were perhaps the most powerful people in much of Europe in 300 B.C., with lands stretching from Anatolia in the East to Ireland in the West. In Britain, at least for a few hundred years after the Roman victories on mainland Europe, the Celts held on to many of their customs, and especially to the distinctive language which has survived today as Welsh. Recently, there has been a revival of bilingual Welsh/English classes in all Welsh schools: BBC Wales airs programs in Welsh, bilingual signs are everywhere, and Welsh is spoken widely throughout the population.

The English came digging for coal, ruining the country. The slag tips became mountains in Wales, and the unrest was dreadful. My mother was 17 in 1926, the year of the Great Strike, when she went off to Cardiff to college to study pharmacy—an odd ambition for a girl from the valley. Peggy suggested to her father that maybe she shouldn't go because the economy was so bad. He wouldn't hear of it, saying he had set the money aside and that she was going to college like the rest of my family. "Have a career my gel," said her Dad, "it will always stand you in good stead."

All the mines closed down on Peggy's first day in college and they were on strike for nine months. Her father opened soup kitchens, got donations to feed people, and helped save the town from starvation. School children did not go home for lunch, and all they had was bread and jam at school. Support for the striking miners eventually came from all over the British Isles. Oxford university students drove buses in London, and everybody rallied around. The Co-op saved the town from starvation during the nine month strike. It took years for the people to pay back the credit given during that awful time, but pay up they did. Being in debt was a dreadful blow to the pride of a Welshman.

University and Working Life

My mother loved her time at university. She studied in the College of Pharmacy within the University of Cardiff. She was a trailblazer of sorts, since there were few female pharmacists then and no women from her small town ever went to university. Pharmacists made drugs and medicines from scratch with pestle and mortar—no pill counting like today! I used to watch my mother in fascination as she measured and made medicines and pills and often thought "what if she makes a mistake and poisons somebody!" But she never did.

In science labs, the students used real drugs to learn dispensing—no sugar or milk! They were taught never to put their fingers near their mouths while preparing drugs because they often worked with dangerous drugs which could be lethal. Peggy always remembered a fellow student sitting in front of her who forgot this important lesson. They were making pills with strychnine, a deadly drug, and the student put her fingers in her mouth. The reaction was immediate as she began thrashing around—a terrifying experience. Luckily, she survived because antidotes were close at hand.

After her studies, Peggy had to go to London to sit her exams. Her brother Cliff was there as well, working at his first job. She stayed at the Russell Hotel and was overwhelmed by it all: a young girl from a small town in Wales going to the big city of London. Cliff took her to see her first theatrical performance, *Old Man River*, at the Drury Lane Theatre, the oldest theatre in London.

After graduation, my mother went back to Mountain Ash and worked in Dr. Hugh Jones' surgery. He used to send all his pneumonia patients to Peggy's father to be cared for.

Doctors had dispensaries in their surgeries, so patients received their medication directly from the doctor. On weekends, Peggy still worked for Mr. Rees, who paid her the grand sum of seven shillings and sixpence for the weekend. Mr. Rees had worked for Boots the Chemist, and advised my mother to apply there for her first big job. He arranged an interview for her with the head office in Cardiff, and she was so nervous she chewed a finger out of her glove! In those days, well brought up women always wore gloves and stockings. Mr. Jones interviewed Peggy and could sense her nervousness, saying, "Well, Miss Davies, you don't have to be nervous with me. Sit down and we'll have a little chat!" It was considered impolite to call somebody by their first name. He was impressed with the experience Peggy already had in her short career. She was 20 years old by now, but he said she was still too young to leave home, and offered her a position in Boots in her hometown until she was 21.

So my mother went to work at Boots in Mountain Ash. She felt so special—working in Boots the Chemist in a white coat, and a woman to boot! People considered Peggy some sort of miracle woman. "Of course, she gets it from her father," everybody said. She gained very good experience working there, and took training to sell Elizabeth Arden cosmetics which were just being introduced to the public. When Peggy let it be known that she would be interested in doing relief work, Mr. Jones said he needed somebody in Tenby, west Wales where all her mother's family came from. One of her mother's brothers was the mayor of Tenby, known as Little England beyond Wales, a gorgeous seaside town with beautiful white, sandy beaches and houses painted in bright colours, reminiscent of Italy's coast. Peggy stayed in "digs," meaning she rented a room in somebody's house.

Peggy didn't have a boyfriend until she was 18 and met Reg Hughes at a hockey club dance. Reg was in the air force and Peggy's friend Gladys Morgan had been going out with him. However, he was stationed at Andover near Salisbury and was always away, so Gladys had another boyfriend, Dennis, in Mountain Ash, who was Catholic. Her family were staunch Baptists and did not approve of Dennis because of his religion. Dennis was at that same dance, and Gladys asked Peggy to take Reg over because Dennis was there. Reg fell for Peggy and she liked him, but it was "three ha'penny love," meaning it was love by correspondence because he only came home sporadically (the cost of a postage stamp was three halfpence). Peggy went out with Reg for four years, but her father never approved. He said Reg would never forget that he was on the parade ground;

he was used to giving orders and Peggy's father said that would not suit her at all.

When Peggy was about 22, she asked for a transfer to Southampton so she could be nearer Andover where Reg was stationed. It was a beautiful, bustling port city with all the big ships coming to call. She shared a house with two other girls who were hairdressers. The owner of the house was a stewardess on the Empress of Britain and she had a maid who cooked for them and generally looked after them.

My Mother Meets My Father

One day Peggy was travelling back from work on the tram and reading a letter from her friend Gladys. She was smiling to herself as she was reading, and felt someone staring at her. She looked up and saw a gorgeous man sitting opposite, smiling with her. Peggy was so embarrassed she did not know where to look, but thought, "boy, I like him." Peggy got off at her stop and watched the tram as it drove away, wondering if she would ever see him again. He was watching her too, and tipped his homburg hat. At that moment, Peggy decided she was not going to marry Reg, to whom she was engaged at the time—she was going to marry the man on the tram. And so she did.

Peggy kept thinking about him, and two evenings later when she was on the tram going home, she saw him outside walking with a friend. He saw her as well, left his friend, and came running after the tram. He jumped on the tram, sat two seats in front of Peggy, and when the conductor came along to collect his ticket, he said he wanted the same colour ticket Peggy had. They both got off at the same stop. He asked her to go to the pictures with him, and they met a couple of hours later after dinner. Peggy had no recollection of the movie at all, only that he spent the movie looking at her while she pretended she didn't notice! All of a sudden, he asked her what her name was. She told him to make a guess. He said, "I'm hoping it's going to be Peggy. It's such a pretty name." He couldn't believe that was her name! Then he said, "Can you guess my name?" Peggy said, "It's got to be Jack." They were astounded.

My parents were married soon after in a registry office during Peggy's lunch time, as neither wanted a big church wedding. Shortly after, the couple went back to Wales so Jack could meet Peggy's parents. It was mutual admiration from the first moment! I was born a year later, and we continued living in Southampton. My father made rapid progress with H.J. Heinz and got frequent promotions. One of these promotions led to a move to Bristol, where my sister Angela was born.

Peggy only had seven wonderful years with the most vibrant, loving, and full of the joy of living person she had ever known. He taught her a great deal about the big world outside Wales.

Tessa with her parents, Peggy and Jack, 1934.

Chapter Two

My Father, Jack Osbourne Durling

Tessa's great-grandfather, Charles Osborn, born in 1839. He served with the British army in India and Burma, 1858–1866. He met and married Mary Agnes Shepherd (nee Florence) in India, and a daughter, Florence was born in Rangoon, Burma. He later taught military training at Eton college in England.

My father was born in London May 16, 1905, the youngest of five children, and he had two brothers and two sisters. His father, Edward Durling, had been with the British army in India and among other things was a tobacconist. Apparently he left the family when my father was quite young and totally disappeared from their lives. His mother Lucy died at age 49 of chronic nephritis when my father was eight years old.

My grandmother's father was Charles Osborn (I have no idea why the spelling of the name changed with my father's birth) who was with the British army in India and Burma for 8 years. According to his service records, it took him 3 months to sail from England to India in 1858 in time for the Delhi Mutiny. His regiment, The King's Rifles, 60th Foot, actually marched from India to Burma! He met his future wife, Mary Agnes Shepherd (nee Florence), in India. She was a widow with one child, and I can only presume her husband must have also been with the army and died there. Charles was honourably discharged after 21 years of service, and became a Chelsea Pensioner. He then taught military training at the famous British public school Eton College, and, according to the 1881 census, lived in the headmaster's lodge with his family of 10. There is a well-known saying that the battles of England were won on the playing fields of Eton. I like to think that maybe he played a role somehow in training some of England's famous generals!

Lucy Osborn, born in 1872, Tessa's paternal grandmother. She married Edward James Durling in Darenth, Kent in 1892 and died at the age of 49 of chronic kidney disease. This portrait of her was painted on porcelain, a custom among comfortably off Victorians.

The Durlings have Lord Horatio Nelson in their family tree. My great-uncle Arthur Edgar Durling married Annie Baker Suckling, a descendant of the famous admiral, one of England's greatest heroes who died in the Battle of Trafalgar defending his country against Napoleon. My father's brother Arthur married Dorothy Tollemache, descended from the Earl of Dysart, a former owner of Ham House in Richmond, England, which now belongs to the National Trust. The Tollemache family were also brewers and Tolley's Breweries still exist today in England. A branch of the Tollemache family owns Helminghall Hall in Suffolk. Dorothy was Auntie Tolley to us and was a wonderful lady who died at 49 of brain cancer. Her daughter, my cousin Pauline, died at exactly the same age of the same illness. Pauline was an architect, artist, and designer of furniture and had her own program on BBC. Her brother John emigrated to Australia. Family legend has it that John wanted to be a ballet dancer. His father, Uncle Arthur, would not hear of it and sent him to Australia at the age of 21 where he bought a sheep station. We know John emigrated to Australia, but the rest of the story might be a figment of someone's imagination!

Uncle Arthur himself was a highly successful businessman, a director of Dunlop Rubber Company responsible for the Middle East. He used to tell many stories of his experiences there dealing with Arabs and eating sheep's eyes! I visited his beautiful Georgian house in Kent and was amazed at all the Arabian carpets which covered the floors, walls, and ceilings, gifts he received from his Arab clients. He was also a colonel in the British army stationed in Hungary during World War II. He married a second time to Jane, an American heiress who died of cancer. His third wife was Betty, his secretary, who looked after him in his final years.

My father's eldest brother Charles was equally successful. He emigrated to the United States at the age of 21 and made his fortune in real estate. He wrote a book of poetry called Memento and was friends with some of the Hollywood stars of that era, namely Merle Oberon and Helen Hayes. His first marriage to Gwen Dehnicke produced two sons, Roy and John (Bunch). I was particularly close to Roy because he had known my father—my only link to him. Charles' second marriage was to Gertrude who was 10 years older than he was and a wealthy woman. Charles spent his later years travelling around the world on the Queen Elizabeth II occupying a penthouse suite which cost $125,000 a trip! The last time I saw him was in Florida at the age of 87. He still retained a strong English accent, and when he met our youngest son Jason who was eight years old at the time, he said, "So you are German, aren't you?" He was very anti-German, as were all the Durlings, who never forgave them for the death of my father when he was torpedoed and perished in the Atlantic Ocean during World War II in 1941.

The fact that my mother was Welsh did not sit well with my father's English family. The English have always tended to look down on the Welsh, Irish, and Scots, considering themselves somewhat superior. The Durling family was no exception. Nevertheless, I have traced back the roots of both sides of my family for hundreds of years, and they have probably been in Britain since before William the Conqueror. Both the Osborn and Durling names are recorded in the Domesday Book, so they are English to the core and proud of it.

Many people are confused about the difference between British and English. British means being English plus either Irish, Welsh, or Scottish. If one side of your family is English and the other side is one of the other members of Great Britain, then you are British, as in my case; if both sides of your family are English, then you are English. The English and Welsh cultures are very different, and I feel privileged to have been brought up in both. Experiencing "both sides" from a very early age has no doubt contributed to my lifelong curiosity about other cultures.

My memories of my father are very vague. According to my mother, he was good-looking, six foot four, with dark hair and laughing brown eyes. He had a wonderful sense of humour and was a great mimic. He was the sort of person everyone noticed when he entered a room. I do remember playing "monkeys" with him and going to the zoo, and I remember when he came home after he had been torpedoed a second time. He climbed through the window of our house in the middle of the night because the front door was locked. He had grown a beard and looked worn and haggard. He seemed like a stranger and I felt afraid when he left again and thought he might never come back. He was torpedoed three times altogether. He was quite an adventurer, having travelled around the world by boat three times by the time he was 20 years old. He always said he was "a Jack of all trades and master of none" because of the many different jobs he had, among them a "Bobby" in the London Metropolitan Police Force.

He was an accomplished artist who could sketch anything and built model ships and furniture. An artistic streak runs in every generation of the Durling family, although I am not sure if it comes from the Osborns or the Durlings. I have always regretted that my mother left behind my father's model of the Mayflower ship when we moved to Canada. I only have one picture he painted which has travelled with me everywhere. My father was an avid sailor and equestrian and his brother Arthur was a master of the fox hunt. I remember my aunts Florence and Margaret showing us a family photo album filled with people on horses. At the age of three I had my own pony and my father had a very high spirited stallion called "Satan" which only he could ride!

When Jack married my mother, he settled down and put all his energy into his job with H.J. Heinz & Co. He was in marketing and actually developed the idea of baby food as we know it today, inspired by my birth, I expect! He would have been 28 at the time and rose rapidly through the company. No doubt, if he had lived, he would have been as successful as his brothers were. Howard Heinz gave my sister and me silver christening cups (even though we were never christened!). My cup now belongs to our oldest grand-daughter Alexandra and is in New Zealand.

Chapter Three

My Childhood

According to an old English saying, "Thursday's child has far to go." I was born Tessa Osbourne Durling on Thursday, July 12, 1934 in Southampton, England and indeed I have travelled far! My parents recounted many times the fierce thunderstorm and torrential rain that heralded my arrival. My sister Angela was born when I was three and I was sent to stay with my father's two sisters, Aunt Florence and Aunt Margaret. They were successful business women, quite unusual at the time, and were always beautifully dressed in the latest styles. Like all the Durlings, they were tall, dark, and good-looking. Auntie Florence had been married but her husband was supposedly sent to jail accused of embezzlement, or so the story goes. She subsequently remarried and her second husband mys-

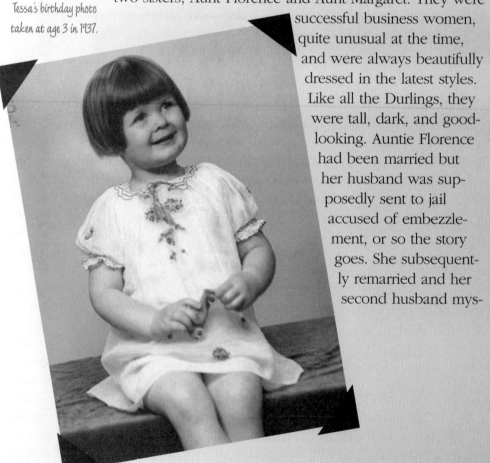

Tessa's birthday photo taken at age 3 in 1937.

teriously disappeared, never to return. Aunt Margaret, on the other hand, never married—her fiancé was killed in World War I.

> While I was staying with them, they wrote the following letter to my mother, which gives a good idea of what kind of child I was.

Dear Peggy:

Just a few reports on your daughter Tessa. I thought you had sent a shy little girl to us but bless my soul she is always in the front row when there is anything doing!

We took her over to the pier yesterday afternoon to see Clown Sunshine and Wendy at the piano. After the clown who, by the way, is a nice, clean, respectable local man, had done his opening song, he asked for some little girls to go on the stage and talk to his boy Jerry (he is a ventriloquist). Eight girls ages 6 to 10 went up and after two minutes had passed, Tessa suddenly decided she would like to go up. So up she went much to the amusement of the audience! When the clown saw her coming he said 'here comes another little girl but she is late.' He then put the others to one side to deal with Tessa, asked her some questions which she answered and he then gave her a stick of rock (peppermint candy). Wendy helped her down the stage and you never saw such confidence in all your life.

Today at meal time she told me I was speaking with my mouth full! This afternoon we went to Peggy's school sports and she did enjoy it. We then went to Clacton to tea and had tea on the pier. Tessa had her tea beautifully. The only thing she could not do was suck her milk *through a straw. She had a good try though— likes to try everything once.*

If the weather is too cold for the beach we go for a walk or do something to occupy the time. Tessa takes to everything and thoroughly enjoys herself. She is such a little wriggler though we can get her to stand still!

Love Florrie.

Daily Life before the War

Our life before the war was typically upper middle class. When I was three, I learned to swim and ride my pony, went to ballet, tap dancing, and elocution lessons. I was so proud of my red tap shoes with their satin red ribbons, but I could never quite master the art of tap dancing. Nevertheless, I was fascinated by the sound of the clicking metal as I tried to learn the intricate steps. We lived in a large house with a garden like a small park and had a dog called Bonzo, a big pond with huge goldfish, and a giant tortoise called Alfred that we used to ride around the garden. Doreen, our maid and nanny, looked after us most of the time and, typical of that era, we saw our parents for meals and bedtime. My parents were in amateur theatre, and I remember being on stage with them during summers at Weymouth, playing an angel in *Sleeping Beauty*, a Roundhead soldier, and a policeman in *Teddy Bear's Picnic*. I can still remember how important I felt blowing a policeman's whistle!

Every Christmas we went to see a pantomime, a cherished English tradition. Our favourite was *Peter Pan*, but *Jack and the Beanstalk* came a close second. Of course, there were no such things as television and videos, and instead Saturday morning was spent at the pictures—it only cost us sixpence! Black and white newsreels showing Nazi soldiers goose-stepping down the streets kept us in touch with what was happening on the battlefronts during the war. The first movie I remember was *The Wizard of Oz* and how terrified I was when the Wicked Witch appeared. Children were allowed to go to adult movies, and I've never forgotten *None but the Lonely Heart* starring Cary Grant, which I saw with my mother who cried buckets of tears all the way through. I must have only been five years old, but Tchaikovsky's music impressed me forever.

Books were everything to us, and I even wrote and illustrated little stories for my sister. We would write our own plays and put on shows for anyone willing to watch. My father had high hopes for his two daughters whom he adored. He wanted us to have the best of everything—education, travel, and eventually finishing school in Switzerland. He dreamed about taking us to our first dance.

Summers

Our summers were spent with my Welsh grandparents in Aust, Somerset where we got up to all kinds of mischief. My grandparent's cottage was quite a contrast to our own home. There was no running water, so rain water was collected in a barrel in the backyard and used for cooking and washing. We had our weekly bath in a tin tub on the kitchen table in front of the fireplace. To my horror, my grandmother also drowned kittens in the rain barrel! It seems there was a proliferation of the feline creatures, and this was the most humane way of controlling the population.

My grandmother cooked on a large fireplace; she had no stove or refrigerator that I can remember.

Every morning she furiously cleaned the fireplace with black polish until it gleamed. The toilet, an outhouse, was outside down the lane a couple of cottages away, and was probably a forerunner of today's "organic" toilets. My grandfather regularly took out the bucket with its contents and spread them on the garden to act as fertilizer. Even as a child I thought the whole procedure rather disgusting. If we had to go to the bathroom in the middle of the night, we had a chamber pot under our beds, nowadays sold as decorative pots in antique shops. There was no such thing as central heating, so we used brass pans with long wooden handles filled with hot coals or hot water bottles to warm up our beds at night. Of course, we took out the pans before we got into the deliciously warm bed!

We had lots of friends who lived on nearby farms. We went birds' nesting in the hedges, collecting all kinds of interesting birds' eggs. It was always so exciting to find a nest with newly laid eggs. We blew out the egg by pricking either end with a pin and then placed it carefully in a box lined with cotton wool to add to our collection. We chased the bulls in the farmer's field and got a great kick out of the farmer chasing us. We fed piglets milk with a baby's bottle, and watched my grandmother catch a chicken, wring its neck, pluck its feathers, and then cook it for dinner. I used to visit the Kingscott bakery and watch with fascination as they slapped and kneaded the dough into loaves of bread and thrust them into giant, hot ovens. Then I went on delivery rounds with one of the Kingscott boys in his van filled with the delicious aroma of newly baked bread and sneaked a crust or two. Everywhere we went, we stopped and chatted and found out the latest gossip.

We were not allowed soft drinks or candy, but we stole money out of my grandmother's worn black purse and went to the village store where we bought our favourite drink and hid in a telephone box to drink it. I don't know if my poor grandmother ever knew. We played with hoops, like today's hula hoops, only we rolled them with a stick. We particularly enjoyed rolling out the hoop as some poor unsuspecting person on a bike with a basketful of milk bottles came down the hill. The hoop crashed into them and the victim flew off the bike as bottles scattered everywhere! We then went into gales of laughter and ran off.

In my more serious moments, I helped my grandfather in his garden and walked miles to the beach on the banks of the River Severn picking up driftwood to fuel his fire. My grandfather was a remote, stern man who said very little, and our treks to the beach were mostly silent. I picked peas and beans, blackberries, black currants, and rhubarb which my grandmother baked into delicious pies and jams. She also made a potent wine out of dandelions. She taught me how to knit clothes for my dolls, and accompanied us to Baptist chapel three times on Sundays. Bible classes were boring, and for fun we threw hymn books at each other!

Chapter Four

Growing Up as a Child of War: 1939–1945

World War II totally dominated my childhood and forever changed my destiny. I was five years old when the war started on the morning of September 3, 1939. Many efforts had been made by then Prime Minister Neville Chamberlain to avert war by peaceful means. The conditions for the Second World War were sown by the Treaty of Versailles (1919–1920) which had taken away parts of Germany as reparation at the end of the First World War, or the Great War. I have subsequently learned from my husband Martin that Germany was in a desperate state of massive unemployment, sowing the seeds for the rise of Adolf Hitler. To his credit, Hitler created jobs by undertaking huge road building projects, which today are still the best in the world.

The German people never forgave the fact that so much of their territory had been taken away following World War I. Adolf Hitler promised to take back what belonged to them, even though he was Austrian and not German. In March 1936, Hitler took back the Rhineland. He took advantage of the civil war in Spain to test his weapons and methods of warfare by bombing the town of Guernica in April 1937. Two years later, on March 11, 1938, German troops marched into Austria. Hitler then demanded a part of Czechoslovakia called the Sudetenland; however this had never been a part of German territory. When the Czechs refused to give in, so did Hitler.

Hitler invaded Poland on September 1, 1939. Britain and France declared war two days later. Hitler continued his march across Europe—Denmark, Norway,

Belgium, Holland, France, and Luxembourg all fell in rapid succession. Britain now stood alone. In the meantime, Neville Chamberlain resigned and Winston Churchill became Prime Minister. The threat of invasion was imminent, and Britain prepared for the onslaught with a series of anti-invasion measures. Beaches were mined, road directions signs were removed, blackouts began, car radios were banned, gas masks were distributed, and air raid warnings were tested. In 1940, London became the target of severe bombing. It was all but destroyed by fire-bombs, but St. Paul's Cathedral miraculously survived even though it was entirely ringed by fire and smoke. Incendiary bombs and V1 and V2 rockets continued until 1944, severely damaging Britain's historic cathedral towns and cities.

English Girl, German Boy

Poison gas had been used in the First World War, so there was a very real chance that it might be used again. Testing our gas masks was part of our daily routine. We had to keep them by our sides or around our necks all the time. I still remember the smell of the rubber as we practised breathing with them, and the piece of tissue paper fluttering at the bottom of the mask to show that air was going through as we breathed in and out. Small children had helmets and babies were put in large containers so they were completely covered.

Black heavy curtains hung on all the windows which were taped with white paper to prevent glass shattering. At night aircraft could see city lights from miles away, so lighting restrictions were imposed to make life more difficult for enemy bombers. Houses had to mask doors and windows so that no light was visible from outside, street lights and shop lights had to be turned off, the headlights of cars and even bicycles had to have special covers. It was very scary walking outside

English Girl, German Boy

when everything was so black! To add to the darkness, coal fires caused a heavy layer of smog to hang in the air covering our faces and everything else with black soot. Every now and then the blackness was pierced by yellow searchlights criss-crossing the sky, trapping enemy fighters in their beams. The war became all too vivid one day when a German airplane was shot down and crashed into a hill next to us. We watched it as it burned and wondered what happened to the German inside. To us, Germans were monsters and we were reminded every day of the evil German empire. The greatest fear was that one day they would be on our doorstep.

Almost from the start of the war, beaches in these areas were planted with mines, barbed wire and other obstacles, so swimming, paddling or playing on the sands were out of the question. From time to time, areas of Britain, especially along the coast, were closed to visitors. In April 1944, all civilians (except those who lived there) were banned from a coastal belt, 10 miles in depth, stretching all along the coast from The Wash to Land's End.

At the beginning of the war, enemy aircraft activity was confined to attacks on shipping in the English Channel, so Seaton, Devonshire where we went to boarding school, was right in the line of enemy flights. I dreaded the sound of the air raid warning. It wailed over and over again. My stomach still turns if I hear a similar sound. Night after night, shortly after the warning, we were woken up out of our sleep and trudged down to our windowless, dark, underground shelter. Then came the drone of enemy aircraft as wave after wave flew overhead, and the suspense of waiting for bombs to drop, hoping we would not be a target. I was so terrified that I was sick to my stomach every time there was an air raid. When the "all clear" sounded, back we would all go to our beds, hoping we could sleep the rest of the night. In 1940, the Battle of Britain waged ferociously over our heads. There were constant dogfights and planes plunged into the English Channel next to us, streaming fire and smoke.

Before the war started, we lived in Bristol and I went to kindergarten at Hampton House school. However, Bristol was an important port city and my parents decided we should move to our grandparents' cottage in Aust, about half an hour outside Bristol, when it became too dangerous to stay there. If Britain was going to be invaded, the invaders would obviously land somewhere on the coast, almost certainly in the south or east where we were. Our house in Bristol was bombed and totally destroyed and ironically, the night we moved to Aust, 48 bombs fell in the fields around my grandparents' house. It was unimaginably terrifying as we huddled under the stairs hearing wave after wave of bombs dropping. As usual, I was sick to my stomach and my grandmother decided pickled onions would help! As the air raid warning sounded, out came the pickled onions. To this day, I can't stand the sight or smell of them. While we stayed inside, my grandmother went outside in the open, saying she felt better being outside. I could never understand why. Perhaps it was because she did not want to be crushed under rubble.

Eventually, German and Italian prisoners-of-war worked on the farms in my grandmother's village, and we often wondered what would happen if they escaped over the farm walls. We were warned constantly to be on our guard. Picking up objects off the ground, especially if they were shiny, was strictly forbidden. They could be some sort of bomb or grenade, although it became a child's hobby to collect pieces of shrapnel in the ruins. Our sky was dotted with barrage balloons which were supposed to prevent airplanes from flying low, and every now and then, silver aluminium foil strips would rain down and litter the countryside. These strips were dropped by aircraft to cause interference with the radar system.

Ironically, my father liked Germany, and he and my mother visited there two months before the war broke out in September 1939. My mother remembered all the signs of pending war, especially the parades of Hitler's brown-shirted soldiers. They were in Hamburg, and brought us back dirndl dresses. When war broke out, my father felt strongly that it was his duty to volunteer to fight against Hitler who was marching his way across Europe and threatening to invade Britain. He joined the Merchant Navy as a chief radio officer, which meant he was in charge of communications on his ship. The Merchant Navy transported food, ammunitions, and other goods through the dangerous U-boat infested waters of the Atlantic. He also went to Africa, but his trips were top secret and he could never disclose his final destination.

On October 17, 1939, he wrote a letter to us from his ship:

Dear Tessa & Angela

Daddy's ship has just arrived in Gibraltar, there are lots of monkeys living here, funny little ones and so friendly that the people feed them every morning. Daddy's so sorry he can't get home but hopes you will write him a nice letter, perhaps you could draw him a picture of a house. Be good girls and nice to Mummy when she comes to see you. (We were living with our grandmother in Aust while our mother worked in Bristol). Yesterday I saw some great big fish swimming in the water, their name is porpoise. Lots of love and a big kiss each from Daddy.

I saved three other letters but they are undated with no ship's name and no indication of where the ship was; no doubt this was for security reasons.

Dear Tessa,

Thank you for your nice letter. I am glad to hear that you are being a happy little girl.

Our cat hasn't caught any mice yet. In the water here there are lots of fish and when we throw bread to them, there is a terrific rush to see who can get there first! Some little birds came to see us the other day and one had a nice red breast. Daddy will be pleased when he can come home and see you. Thank you for looking after Angela and being a good girl for Mam Mam. Love to you all, from your Daddy

---

Darling Tessa,

What do you think; we now have another cat on the ship. The man who cooks our dinner looks after it. He hasn't thought of a name for it yet, what would you call him? One of the men on the ship asked me if I worried about Angela, I said of course not, I have a clever little girl named Tessa to look after her. Here is a picture I drew of a house, can you do it? God bless you my dear and give Angela a big kiss for me and one for yourself. Daddy

To my lovely girls Tessa and Angela

I was so glad to hear that you are being good and having a nice time. Our cat Blackie has been chasing birds all day long but never catches any. I went on another ship the other day and saw a lovely monkey. He was so sweet and lived on the ship with the men. They have lots of fun with him and he climbs everywhere. I went for a swim in the sea, it was lovely and warm. I swam under the water and caught another man by his toe; he was so surprised and said oh——! When I come home, if I have time, I will take you to tea in Bristol and listen to the band. Are you learning a lot at school? Can Angela ride her bicycle yet? I went to see a man the other day and saw his little girl fast asleep in bed with two little dollies. I kissed her hand but she didn't wake up. She has a big doll's house to play with but she didn't have a doggie like Bonzo and no little sister. She was 4 years old. She wasn't big enough to go to school.

Love from Daddy to his beautiful girls and give Mummy a big kiss for me.

During the war, my mother and father corresponded with the Huntley family, Americans living in

Baltimore, whom Jack had befriended and visited frequently during the war while on his transatlantic runs.

Following are excerpts of a letter from Jack to the Huntleys on January 7, 1941. His ship was the S/S Waynegate, somewhere at sea.

Dear Huntleys,

We are due to arrive in the UK in about a week so that, if you receive this letter, you will know that we did arrive! Scrap iron in itself is never a very pleasant cargo but on arrival in New York you can imagine our feelings when we were told to load 600 tons of high explosives, and yet it is amazing how adaptable one can become, already its presence is almost forgotten.

I was fortunate enough to have Kmas in New York and had Kmas dinner with my brother (Charles) who I am glad to say is back in the fold of his family. He has a charming house way out in the wilds of Connecticut, and on Kmas day we were able to sit outside the house warmed by sunshine. It was grand seeing my nephews; one is almost as tall as me.

I have started "Mrs. Minniver." I read a little every night before sleeping. It's a delightful book reminding me of all the joys of family life and, for a brief moment, takes my mind away from war's unpleasantness.

By the way, isn't the news about Libya charming? I bet Jack (Huntley) is tickled to death; probably he has put an inch on his chest with pride in being British! Maybe I shall have next Kmas at home in peace.

The weather has been phenomenal. We had one stormy day which was very bad and carried away one lifeboat. Of course the old lady (the ship) is rolling heavily and right now it is not easy to write. However the trip I dreaded hasn't turned out so bad after all (so far).

English
Girl,

German
Boy

In August 1941, Admiral Sir Percy Noble, Commander-in-Chief, Western Approaches, in praise of the Merchant Navy, wrote that:

> They know these men, that the Battle of the Atlantic means wind and weather, cold and strain and fatigue, all in the face of a host of enemy craft above and below, awaiting the specific moment to send them to death. They have not even the mental relief of hoping for an enemy humane enough to rescue nor the certainty of finding safe and sound those people and those things they love when they return to homes, which may have been bombed in their absence. When the Battle of the Atlantic is won, as won it will be, it will be these men and those who have escorted them whom we shall have to thank.

Food Rationing

Food shortages were a major problem. Most of Britain's food and raw materials were imported from other countries by sea. The British Isles is a collection of islands and cannot possibly supply everything for its population. This posed a real danger when the Germans put Britain under siege, using U-boats to sink merchant ships bringing in oil, food, petrol, wood, and many other vital materials. Losses were huge—over half of all the British merchant ships (including my father's) at the beginning of the war had been sunk by the end of it. Britain came closer to losing the war to U-boats than in any other way.

The government provided everyone with a ration book. The Adult book was a buff colour, the Baby's book was green, and the Junior book was blue. Butter and bacon or ham were the first goods to be rationed in January 1940, only 4 ounces of each per person per week; then sugar, 12 ounces a week. In March

1940, only 1s 10d worth of meat per person per week was allowed. By Christmas 1940, tea had been rationed to 2 ounces a week and sugar was cut to 8 ounces. After Christmas, there were no more bananas or fresh or tinned fruit. Later shortages led to milk rationing.

As well as the coupons for specified rationed goods, each ration book contained a number of points coupons. While some items were "put on points," the points coupons could be used to buy any items on points. Bread was not rationed and nor were some other foods such as potatoes and other root vegetables. People were encouraged to use every inch of their gardens to grow their own produce and raise animals, including chickens, ducks, geese, and rabbits. I don't ever remember having fresh eggs during the war, only dried powdered eggs. We ate a lot of fish because we lived by the sea, and lots of rabbit, but very little other meat.

We were luckier than most people because of the Huntley family. They sent us wonderful parcels full of all the goodies we couldn't get in Britain, and it was always magical when parcels from America arrived with the postman. With eager anticipation we ripped off the paper and chocolates, tinned fruit, ham, clothes, and silk stockings for my mother spilled out. I'll always remember the two dolls we named Jane and Elizabeth whose eyes opened and shut! Food parcels from the United States made such a huge difference to British lives; they were forever grateful for their generosity. Rationing continued until 1953, long after the war was over. In post-war Britain, food and other goods were still very scarce.

In January 1941, my mother wrote to Mrs. Huntley describing some of the hardships in Britain.

It is hard to get very much at all. We are able to get enough to eat but most of our luxuries have been cut out. Sweets in this small place are practically non-existent. It's very amusing to hear Tessa work out when each shop is likely to have a little stock. She usually manages to get a share when a shop receives its monthly quota. Go into the shop half an hour later and it looks as if it had been besieged by vultures. It's absolutely bare for another month. This coming week we are only going to be allowed one shilling and six pence worth of meat for children over six and adults. That means my meat allowance will be three shillings and nine pence for the week. We get 2 oz. of butter per person now but I am told it will be 1 oz. very soon. We have not seen bananas for weeks and no oranges since Christmas. However, we are far from starving and luckily I had some tinned fruit stored.

Last night was the first time we had an "alert" sounded in this area. The house was vibrating so badly that we sat up until 2 a.m. until the "raiders passed" sounded or the "dying pig" as the children have named it. Our dear Bristol has been having a terrible time and has been set on fire like London. Still, life goes on, business goes ahead, people get to their offices on time, shops carry on. Friends in Bristol write and tell me shops are springing up in the weirdest of places. The house we lived in is no more. In spite of all the bombing and destruction, transport is very little affected. Hitler is up against a tough job now he has met the British and he will never win.

Writing on February 17, 1941, my mother described my father's homecoming and thanked the Huntleys for all the gifts they sent.

He was home for three weeks this time before leaving for Freetown, Sierra Leone. He was so disappointed he was not returning to the U.S. and was looking forward to seeing them all and going shopping for food and dresses. I think he would have spent a great deal of his time in the shops. He even took our measurements for dresses. He tells me it's quite unique for a man to go shopping for ladies wear in America. That strikes me as funny, because in England it's quite a common sight.

He was always bringing me home some surprise. I am glad you agree about him being devoted to us, and it's nice to hear that he speaks so fondly of us. He is a darling and this week we are missing him terribly.

He couldn't believe the amount of foodstuffs we are short of. It was quite a problem trying to satisfy that colossal appetite of his. Two shilling and eleven pence worth of meat doesn't go very far. However, we helped it out with rabbit, fish, and sausages. It is difficult to adjust oneself to the everlasting economies. But we jog along without the suet, fat for cooking, fruits, butter, meat, etc. We are a long way off starving, it is just getting used to doing without things we have been spoiled with, and having to use our brains to plan meals. Lack of fruit is the only thing that worries me because the children have to do without it and I have always given them a good fruit diet. However, even they are bursting with good health and spirits so I can't even moan about their lack of fruit!

When Jack told the girls about the suits you had sent them, they were bitterly disappointed to think they won't get them now. I was upset too to think you had spent such a lot of money and then not to have the pleasure of knowing the children had received them. In this country we can claim compensation for parcels not received, so I wonder if the same can be done in the U.S. Jack was looking forward to seeing Tessa and Angela strutting around in them!

What a jolly Christmas you all must have had. I wonder how long it will be before those days come back to us. It's extraordinary at the moment here. Nothing seems to be happening. No air activity, no sound of a plane. That madman (Hitler) is planning some mischief! People all talk about an invasion, fortunately I never think about it ever happening. I'm not the least bit nervous; I just don't think they could do it. Oh! What a smashup they'll have when they attempt it! I pity the paratroops, if they ever come, what a hot reception we will give them. I really think I could manage a few all on my own.

Still, it's all a very horrible business and the sooner it's over the better for all of us.

Clothing Rationing

Clothes rationing was announced in June 1941. Unlike food rationing, it was not primarily brought in as a result of shortages of raw materials, but rather to release factories and factory workers for war work. There were no separate ration books available, but people were told to use the spare coupons in their food ration books for the first year. Separate clothing ration books were first issued in June 1942.

Rationing was extremely tight. The following four-year plan for a woman's and man's wardrobe shows how little people could buy.

Woman's Wardrobe:

First Year   1 pair shoes, 6 pairs stockings, 10 ounces wool or 2.5 yards material, 1 suit, 1 overcoat, 2 slips, 1 blouse

Second Year   1 pair shoes, 6 pairs stockings, 8 ounces wool or 2 yards material, 1 silk dress, underwear 2 or 3 pairs, brassiere and girdle (2 or 3 pairs)

Third Year   2 pairs shoes, 6 pairs stockings, 4 ounces wool or 1 yard material, 1 Jacket, 1 skirt, 2 cotton or silk dresses, 2 slips, 1 pair of corsets, 6 handkerchiefs

Fourth Year   1 pair shoes, 6 pairs stockings, 6 ounces wool or 1.5 yards material, 1 woolen dressing gown, underwear 2 or 3 pairs, corset or brassiere (2 or 3 pairs), 6 handkerchiefs

Man's Wardrobe:

First year   1 pair boots or shoes, 6 pairs socks, 1 suit, 1 overcoat, collars, ties or handkerchiefs

Second Year   1 pair boots or shoes, 6 pairs socks, 1 pair corduroy trousers, 3 shirts (silk or cotton), 2 pairs pants, 2 vests, 1 pair gloves

Third Year   1 pair boots or shoes, 5 pairs socks, 1 suit, 1 pullover, 1 pair pyjamas

Fourth Year   1 pair boots or shoes, 6 pairs socks, 1 overcoat or raincoat, vests, collars, ties or handkerchiefs, 3 shirts, 2 pairs of pants

Clothes rationing for children was a nightmare for parents, because little thought was given to children growing out of their clothes. Clothes were patched and passed on or exchanged, and adults' castoffs were remade into dresses or coats. Women had to be very resourceful and handy with the needle to cope with the rationing.

One of the last photos of Tessa and her family together, March 1941, exactly one month before her father was killed. They are walking along the seafront in Seaton, Devon. Note the barricades and sandbags in preparation for an invasion by the Germans.

At the end of 1942, older children received extra clothing coupons, the amount depending on when they were born. The government had two mottos: "make do and mend" (patch and mend existing clothes), and "sew and save" (alter old clothes to make new ones). Children of the war grew up with a "waste not, want not" mentality—we never threw anything away if it needed fixing; we fixed it because there was no other alternative.

English Girl,

German Boy

Chapter Five

My Father is Killed

On March 19, 1941, exactly one month before he was killed, my father wrote the following letter to Mrs. Huntley.

Dear Mrs. Huntley,

Herewith a brief journal of recent events in the Durling ménage. Firstly, about five weeks ago, I sailed for Sierra Leone, West Africa but was unfortunate enough to be torpedoed 450 miles off the Irish coast and after various experiences eventually arrived home for special leave. I am now reaching the end of my leave and am due for another attempt. This time I hope it will be in your direction. Chances are quite good of going to the US and I would appreciate a short spell in the security of American waters.

I don't need to tell you that things are pretty tough at home. Personally, I have passed through several phases, depression, fear, etc. but have finally persuaded myself, that if I must die, then I will try and do it cheerfully like a man!!

My family is back in Aust. No place can be safe, therefore it is as well for them to be among people they know and I feel would help them if they needed it. If it were possible I would risk sending them to the States but I don't think passengers are allowed to leave the U.K. I am happy to be back in Aust, where I can forget our troubles for a little while, digging in the garden. We came back yesterday and today the weather gave us a grand welcome and I have been in the garden planting potatoes because I think this vegetable will be one of our main foods in the future.

The children have both had bad whooping cough, an unpleasant complaint, but they are now over the worst. They are tickled to death to be back in Aust and look very happy.

Thank goodness they can't understand how serious things are.

I am afraid I haven't much heart in letter writing these days but maybe I shall see you soon for a good long gossip. In the meantime best wishes to you all.

Writing from Aust on April 14, 1941, my mother wrote the following letter to Mrs. Huntley. My father was killed a week later.

Dear Mrs. Huntley,

You will see by the above address that I am back at our home with the children. It is not an easy thing to live for a length of time in some stranger's house, especially with two high-spirited children. They weren't very happy at Seaton. Tessa, more so than Angela, missed her home life and her little companions, the swing in the garden, the sand-pit, all their toys, etc. which mean so much to little ones.

I had been considering coming back when Jack came back to us thank God after being torpedoed in the Atlantic. The very night he came home the sirens wailed out their warnings and there were enemy planes overhead. One came and machine gunned the house next door and so we made our minds up to come back to Aust where we were surrounded by friends who would help us if trouble came to us. Jack didn't like the idea of me being alone with strangers with the children. They were delighted and have never looked as well as they do since we have been back.

Today, Jack rang me up for our last little chat before sailing again for an unknown destination. It's all very hush-hush. One thing he is certain of, he won't be looking you all up this trip. He is very down-hearted about that. You have no doubt had his letter telling you of his mishap. He has been home six weeks, a lovely long time, but it makes it so much harder to part with him. I pray very hard for him to be brought home again safely.

It's a very strange life we lead these days. I enjoy no social life; there is simply nothing to do. All our friends are either in the Forces or in the civil defence services. Most of my women friends are either evacuated with their children, ambulance driving, or part-time nurses, etc. When they are off duty, I have the children to attend to and our spare time just doesn't fit in.

So I busy myself with growing our vegetables, knitting for Tessa and Angela, and, at the moment, I am cutting out summer dresses for them from my old ones. Material is inferior and anyway expenses have to be cut down because food prices are so high. Honestly though, I get more thrill out of making something out of practically nothing than I do out of something I have bought new.

Last week, Jack and I went into Bristol to do some shopping and also to see for ourselves the damage the raiders had wrought. Oh, Mrs. Huntley, it was heart-breaking to see our beautiful Bristol so dev-astated. The lovely shops were just burnt out shells. We lost our way several times because all our landmarks had been destroyed. But, look-ing over the city from a bridge, one thing struck me as being symbolic. There shining in the afternoon sunshine was what remained of St. Mary-le-port church. Its spire was still standing bravely, its golden cross gleaming as if sending us a ray of hope. Jack caught my glance and he just nodded and said, "That's one thing Hitler can't beat down in us, call it hope if you like, but it's very close to stubbornness." And so we went on to another part of Bristol, when we were overtaken by three ragged little chaps, seats out of their pants, proudly pulling behind them a toy crane, motor car and engine. They had been doing some looting from a bombed, burnt out toy shop. They looked so proud of their treasures, rusty but still wheeling along in grand style——British made you see!

Good Friday night we were shocked by terrific gun barrage. Deep throated guns were firing into the sky making a very pretty display, with shells bursting and flares dropping. We have a kind of ringside seat at Aust; we can see and hear what is going on in Bristol during a raid. It was terrific that night and the next day we heard the result. It was terrible. The wounded were being attended outside the infirmary and working class districts were very badly hit. This isn't war, it's mass murder.

When I read your letter to the children, they were amazed to know that Frances knew the "Muffin Man." Tessa can sing quite well but Angela is the one with the voice. She only has to hear a tune once and without effort she will hum it immediately and remember it.

They attend Sunday school now and they know all the hymns better than I do. They were listening on the radio to the children who were evacuated to Canada and America talking with their parents. They loved it and Angela said "Wish I could go and live there and then I could say "moth-ur-ur" then." That was because I had been giving her a lecture on picking up the Somerset accent. It's amazing how quickly those evacuated children have acquired an American accent. Tell your sewing group their work is so gratefully received by the English people. Your hearts would gladden if you had seen on the films how the children loved trying on the gifts from America.

English
Girl,

German
Boy

With my father's death at the age of 36, our whole world collapsed. I will never forget when my mother received a telegram saying he was missing at sea. She dropped to the floor in a dead faint and I thought she was dead too! I often wondered what it must have been like to die in those cold waters. Did he die instantly or did he bob around in the sea until he could no longer survive? For years I did not know, and only recently got the answer in one of my mother's letters while writing this book. According to survivors, my father and his ship mates were torpedoed as their lifeboat was being lowered into the water. So it was much worse than I thought. His ship "The Empire Endurance" was sunk off the coast of Ireland in the North Atlantic on April 20,1941 by the German U-boat U73 commanded by Helmut Rosenbaum of Leipzig, Germany. The Battle of the Atlantic is the name given the conflicts in the Atlantic Ocean during World War 11. The aim of the Germans was to cut off supplies to Great Britain which, as an island nation, was highly dependent on sea-going trade. The German navy was very successful during the first years of the war and sunk 116 British merchant ships in the first six months of 1941. The SS Athenia was the first passenger ship to be torpedoed in 1939. Ironically, my mother had booked passage on the Athenia but later cancelled because she thought it was too dangerous.His death affected me so much that I went from being right-handed to left-handed and became very withdrawn. My mother wrote this letter on May 4, 1941, telling Mrs. Huntley about my father's death.

Dear Mrs. Huntley,

I feel I must write and write about my darling husband. I don't know how I'm going to live without him, but I know I shall have to carry on for the sake of the two dear children he gave me. I feel I shall never stop crying again. You see yesterday I had a letter from the Marconi Company telling me his ship was sunk by enemy action and that he is not among the survivors landed in this country. I can't, I can't believe it! It's too horrible to really believe. We loved each other so dearly and to think that perhaps never again will I hear his dear voice or see him, is really more than I can bear at the moment. I say perhaps I won't see him again because they seem to think he might be a prisoner or landed in some other country. But the suspense of it, wondering and looking for the postman, is awful.

He wanted to do so much for the children. He often spoke of how proud he would be to take them to their first dance and theatre. He wanted to give them all the joys of being alive and well educated young ladies. But now, what? They will have to go to the village school, I won't be able to send them to the Manor House School any more or to their dancing and elocution lessons. It hurts me so much to see their puzzled faces because they can't go any more. They adored their Daddy and they keep on mentioning things about him which digs deeper into the wounds those swines of Germans have inflicted on me. I dread the years of loneliness ahead of me.

It's wonderful to have the children of course and I will devote my whole life to them. But to have no Jack to discuss things with, not to admire our dresses and the way my hair is set, and not to see the children grown up and share the joys of them growing up. Oh, it's all so empty and futile. Forgive me for writing like this but I know you will understand because I believe you were fond of him too.

I have to go to Bristol tomorrow to see if I can get in touch with any of the survivors. I must know what happened.

When my father was killed, my mother was living in Bristol, England, trying to survive the bombing and cope with rations. She went back to work at Boots the Chemists to earn a living for us. She felt she was fortunate to be able to send us to a private boarding school rather than evacuate us to a family in the country. In many ways, I suppose my sister Angela and I were lucky to be in boarding school in Devon. Thousands of children from the large inner cities such as London and Manchester were evacuated to strangers in safe areas during the war. Most of these children came from poor families and their experiences were not all happy ones. Many of them returned to their families rather than be alone with strangers. Children from wealthier families were sent to friends or relatives in the country.

The American lady who befriended Jack and sent many food parcels to Peggy throughout the war.

At the ages of six and three, we travelled on the train by ourselves from our home in Sidmouth to the school in Seaton in charge of the train conductor. I can still remember the wave of nausea I felt whenever I went on that train. I hated being alone and responsible for my sister. In those days, there was no such thing as bereavement counselors or psychologists to help us deal with the death of our father; we were left alone in a strange environment to cope as best we could with our life-altering loss.

On July 4, 1941, my mother wrote the following to the Huntleys.

Dear Mrs. Huntley,

I am sure you will understand and forgive me for not answering your most comforting letter a little sooner. I have been almost overwhelmed with correspondence dealing with Jack's estate, etc. Although it is an unpleasant business, I really am grateful I had it all to do because it helped me keep my sense of balance, occupied my mind, and enabled me to get through the first few awful weeks.

I have had no further news of him, only the gruesome details, and I feel sure you will not want me to go into all that and so open up the old wounds. All it really amounts to is that the life-boat he was able to get into was torpedoed as it was lowered into the water. That is the Germans' conception of warfare! Kick men when they are down, by God! What they have coming to them is more than I shall ever want to witness! I'm sure they won't find any soft-hearted British to mete out their punishment at the end of this war. They have a different generation to deal with. A generation who suffered through the last war (World War I) and has now been pitch-forked into a war-maddened world. Oh no, the Hun won't get away with it this time!

However, I still hold out faith that my Jack is somewhere and that one of these days I shall hear his dear, happy, joyful voice again and I shall have him to cherish and give all the happiness I can to make up for what he is suffering somewhere now. The children will not accept that Daddy has gone to the "angels." They are so certain he will come back and that gives me the courage to carry on where he left off.

To supplement my pension which is so small in comparison to Jack's income, I have taken a post with the A.R.P. HQ as a telephonist in the message room. That is where all the notifications of air raids are taken. I find it most interesting and most congenial because I have two days a week when I don't have to report for duty which gives me a little spare time to be with the children and see to things at home. The other girls at the office look on me as their lucky mascot because only twice have we had the sirens since I started about 6 weeks ago. That is wonderful compared with the amount of alerts received in Bristol. So I'm hoping my luck holds out.

I am so happy that, after all my worrying, I am able to send the children as boarders to the school Tessa attended in Devon. I still hate parting with them, but I feel I am doing the best for them. When I know they are well cared for and getting a good education, I feel so much more free to do my job. They will be off in September and are very thrilled about it. I do feel that the fact of being together will help tremendously. Doesn't it all seem so wicked that our happy family has been torn asunder? It's all so different to what Jack had planned for us.

I sometimes wonder if I shall ever be able to make a life for myself so that I can be a little bit happy. We were so wrapped up in each other, I never wanted to do anything without Jack and he felt the same. He didn't seem to want to mix with other men and spend his spare time at the club, etc. He never could get home quick enough. If only a miracle would happen and he suddenly walked in or phoned me! I mustn't write this way, it's only wishful thinking and it might make you cry.

I must thank you for the lovely parcel you sent me. I loved it all, so very thoughtful of you. You ask if all the things were what we wanted. Well, tea we manage very well, I seem to get sufficient butter, but spam has proved a marvelous standby and has saved the situation when we were stuck. We love it and, of course, the nestle café and sugar. I would be so grateful if you could manage suet, dried fruits— raisins, prunes, etc., anything in the fruit line. The children were goggle-eyed when the chocolate was unpacked! They hadn't seen so much at one time for ages. You may rest assured everything was very much appreciated.

The children have a birthday on Saturday. Jack always gave them a lovely party and this year I must keep it up. They were very anxious to know if they were having one. Tessa invites the whole village so we have to engage the village hall. About 24 boys and girls are expected. Tessa made out her list and has been very busy today ticking the names off. Angela knows it's all very important but is quite content to let Tessa do the inviting. So the cake has been ordered, we were just lucky enough to order before the quota for the month had been reached. It would have been a catastrophe if I had been too late! They are in bed while I am writing this and both singing "Do you know the Muffin Man?"—what lungs! Now it's only three more days until July 12, Tessa is laboriously counting the days. How wonderful it is to be a child! Everything is such an adventure and so thrilling!

I will most certainly let you have a photograph of us as soon as I can arrange it. I always have the children photographed each birthday. I really must stop now; I have horrid letters to write after this one. I wish all were so enjoyable to write. I hope you will write very soon to me. I feel you belong to one of the happy times of Jack's lifetime. He thought so much of you all and I loved to hear him talk about your way of living and all about your home life.

School Life

Our school was called Manor House, and it had been evacuated from London. My father's family had gone to the same school. When he died, the headmistress very kindly took us in at half the cost. The school was very close to the beach on the English Channel, and I have very strong memories of the iron bars and cement blocks which acted as barriers to prevent people from going on the heavily-mined beaches. I also saw what happened if anyone dared venture there. The funeral procession of two Czech soldiers, their helmets on top of their coffins, passed our school one day—they had been blown up by mines on the beach. It was a sober reminder to us and is a vivid memory to this day.

Mr. Huntley

Even though we were at war, life continued as best it could. Many schools in London and other big cities were badly disrupted because of frequent daylight air raids, although most air raids happened at night. Somehow, we still managed to learn in spite of not having sufficient books and other supplies. I was in Form 1 at the beginning of the war, and was an avid, ambitious student, always at the top of the class. I was also a keen field hockey player and was captain of our team. We played rounders, netball, and tennis. Deportment was an important subject. To achieve the goal of standing and sitting straight, we had to walk around the gym with books on our heads, resulting in gales of laughter as the books slid and fell off our heads! Daily air raid and gas mask practices were part of our school routine, and trips at night to the air raid shelter in the basement of the school were all too frequent.

We were very proud of our leaf green and yellow school uniform, which gave us a sense of identity whenever we were outside the school. Everyone knew we went to Manor House. In wintertime, we wore green tunics with white blouses and yellow and green striped ties and knee socks. We wore heavy green coats with large brimmed felt hats, complete with a yellow and green ribbon and our school coat of arms. We had green blazers with yellow trim and green berets as an alternative to the felt hats. In the summer, we wore green and white gingham dresses and panama hats.

We slept in rows in large dormitories, and for fun had midnight feasts eating whatever we could scrounge or that had arrived in our food parcels. We used to get into lots of trouble if Matron found out; punishment usually meant a smack on the rear end with a slipper or hairbrush. Luckily, I never got caught!

It's surprising to me today how we survived those winters without central heating. We constantly had red, chapped knees and chilblains, inflamed sores or swellings caused by the cold that itched horribly as they healed. We wore knitted gloves with half fingers to try and prevent chilblains, and help prevent scratching. I suffered with them on my toes and fingers all during the war. We also caught every illness going, and my sister and I were always the first in the infirmary. We had measles, mumps, chicken pox, whooping cough, yellow jaundice, and I even had glandular fever. When we had

English girl, German Boy

yellow jaundice (hepatitis), our mother had to push us around in a wheelchair for a month because we were so weak. Every day, the whole school lined up as Matron gave us our vitamin supplements—cod liver oil, malt, Scott's Emulsion, and to keep us regular, syrup of figs (ugh!). Vitamin supplements were vital to keep us healthy because there was such a food shortage and everything was heavily rationed.

Boarding school food, never the best, was boring and monotonous. We never had eggs, milk, cheese, fruit, much meat, or ice cream. The only desserts I remember were treacle pudding, which I hated because it made me thirsty and we were not allowed to drink our water until we had finished our meal. Spotted Dick was a suet type white pudding with raisins and looked like a Dalmatian's coat. Then there was the everlasting blancmange in various colours, bread and butter pudding, and rice pudding. Overcooked boiled vegetables were tasteless and dull. The only relief we had from school food were weekly visits by my mother on Thursdays when she would take us out for a treat.

Ann Hammett was my best friend. Her parents were divorced which was rather shocking in those days, and to my child's mind, this gave her an exotic air. She was different from the rest of us, but so was I because my father had been killed in the war, something I was strangely enough ashamed of. Ann's father must have been quite important because he used to arrive at the school in a large, expensive car. He very kindly included me when he took Ann and her sister Mary out and treated us to ice cream on his weekly visits.

Leisure Activities

War or no war, children had leisure time and found ways to amuse themselves. Older children were very much involved in the war effort. There was a very strong sense of patriotism, and all the British people were encouraged to help their country. Some schools adopted a ship or a military unit, knitted clothes and blankets for men serving, and also collected books and magazines for them. Older children acted as messengers for the local police or fire brigade, worked as telephonists, control room orderlies, or gas-mask assemblers, and filled sandbags or made tea and sandwiches for civil defence workers. Children helped on farms fruit-picking, harvesting, and hop-picking. They collected paper and scrap metal, and chopped wood for old people. Boy Scouts and Girl Guides helped in hospitals and first aid posts, and many joined the Air Training Corps, the Women's Junior Air Corps, or the Boys' Brigades.

In an age of no television, videos, computers, or computer games, radio and movies were our main source of entertainment. Radio encouraged our imaginations because we had to visualize our own pictures as we listened. Every day we eagerly awaited Children's Hour on the BBC between 5 and 6 p.m., and I can still hear Uncle Mac saying "Hello children everywhere!" as he introduced the program. There were readings from classic stories like *Wind in the Willows* and *Great Expectations*, British history, singing, and nature study. We also listened to other programs like *Charlie McCarthy*, a ventriloquist act. When we heard the solemn tones announcing *BBC Calling*, we huddled around the radio to listen to the latest war news and Winston Churchill's rousing speeches. Who could forget his "We shall never surrender" speech? Saturday mornings we went to the cinema and saw cartoons, Judy Garland movies, and ten-minute newsreels showing progress on the war front.

In many of the large cities, bomb sites were children's playgrounds where imaginations held full rein among the ruins. Toys were practically non-existent and were mostly war- related, like tanks and planes. I remember having two dolls and two teddy bears which we played with endlessly. We played board games and card games to pass the time during air raids. For me, books were everything. I especially enjoyed Enid Blyton's stories and Rupert the Bear's adventure books written in comic book form. All during the war, most comics

"Children of an eastern suburb of London, who have been made homeless by the random bombs of the Nazi night raiders, waiting outside the wreckage of what was their home."
September 1940

produced a Christmas annual such as *The Big Top Circus Annual* and *Radio Fun Annual* which were full of stories and pictures.

What my sister and I missed more than anything was a family life. We grew up pretending we had seven brothers, even telling people that they were in boarding school in Switzerland! You can imagine my mother's astonishment when she was asked about her seven sons. We rarely saw cousins, uncles, and aunts, but we did correspond with our cousins in the United States. We occasionally saw our Welsh relatives who lived in England, but our only close relationship was to our mother's parents. We stayed in boarding school throughout the war—a total of six years, most of our childhood.

English Girl, German Boy

Chapter Six

Arrival of the Americans—1942

In a letter my mother wrote on January 30, 1942, she thanked Mrs. Huntley once again for another parcel she sent and talked about how severe the rationing was.

> The only fruit we get is apples and dried fruit is available, but we have to give so many coupons for it. But, in spite of it, we all stay very healthy and free of colds. The children are happy and doing well at school and I go to see them every Thursday. Tessa is still convinced that Daddy is a prisoner. She tells me all her dreams about him; it is very heart-breaking to hear her confident young voice. She misses him so terribly. Angela, being younger, does not realize the loss. I think I am adjusting myself to conditions now and although I miss Jack a hundred times a day, I really think its not quite so painful now. Do you know it will be a whole year in two months' time? It doesn't seem possible. This time last year he was home.

In 1942, the United States finally entered the war after the bombing of Pearl Harbor by Japan. American troops began to arrive in Britain in the build-up to the invasion of Europe. At this point, my mother writes to the Huntleys:

I wonder often how the war will affect you now. I hope with all my heart that all of you will not have to bear the horrors of war as we have known them. For months now, we have been free of air-raids and life seems most tranquil. It's just when we go shopping that we now realize there is a war on and being parted from our men folk. That doesn't even apply to me now. All that anxiety of wondering if the ship was safe has gone. I had to register last Saturday, being 32. I don't suppose I shall be called up, because, apart from having the children, a pharmacist is reserved, because I have filled a man's place.

We have an R.A.F. (Royal Air Force) station near here and there are a number of American and Canadian boys stationed there. I met one from Boston in the bus one day.

Knowing you, I felt I had the right to speak to any American. He was a very nice, young fellow and I invited him to tea, have shown him around the country, and introduced him to some friends. Now he is well able to amuse himself having become very fond of one of my friends.

I always await your letters very eagerly and one should just about be due now. I shall be interested to hear all about your Xmas festivities. I'm afraid ours were very subdued this year but the children had a lovely time. Lots of parties and their godmother took them to the pantomime "Mother Goose." They spent the school holidays at home with my mother and I was able to have almost a week with them.

I do wish this awful war would end. I often wonder if we will ever meet.

English Girl, German Boy

Life got a little better when the Americans opened a naval base not far from us. They used to give Christmas parties for all the children nearby and gave us candies and chewing gum which we never had during the war. Although the Americans were popular with children and women, they were loathed by everybody else, especially British servicemen. American servicemen were often described as "over-sexed, over-paid, and over here." My mother made friends with some of the officers who came to dinner at our house. One special friend was Commander Trudeau Thomas from Baltimore who used to drive us around in his jeep and took us into the forest to cut down a tree for Christmas. It was a beautiful tree, and the only one we had during the war. We made our own Christmas decorations out of coloured paper. I had one Christmas present that year: a second-hand bicycle!

After not receiving any letters from the United States for a few months, a letter finally came. On November 13, 1942 my mother replied.

I wrote to you wondering how your entry into war had affected you, but received no replies. I was so glad to get your letter telling me all about the whole family and its war work. It is hard and tedious work, but this week it heartens one to hear the news of the battle for Egypt and our victory there. At last some result after three weary years of struggle!

I don't know if I told you before that I am now settled in this flat. It's very pleasant and so nice to have my home around me once more. I became so weary of living in other people's houses and nothing to do with my spare time. I like to busy myself about the house and poke around in the garden. It's true I know I only have a 2x4 garden now, but it's about all I have the time for. It should look very pretty in the spring with its wallflowers, tulips, and forget-me-nots. It's so nice too for the children.

They spent four weeks of the summer holiday with me. We had great fun swimming and picnicking on the beach. They are growing up now and are great company for me. Tessa is at last getting over the shock of losing Daddy and is becoming her old sunny self again. It's grand to see that wistful look disappearing. Her headmistress advised me to let her take up music, so this term she has started to learn the piano. She loves it and seems to show an aptitude. Angela of course is as saucy as ever and very amusing. Tessa is a fully fledged Brownie now and Angela wrote telling me this "I can skip eleven times now with some-body turning the rope."

There are lots of Americans here now. Quite a few of the officers are in the town. I always wonder where they come from and always hop-ing I might meet somebody who knows you. If anybody you know should come over, do put them in touch with me. I would be so happy to return some of the hospitality you showed Jack.

Well, life rolls on just the same. It's a little more peaceful now. Hitler doesn't seem to get time to bomb us very much now. It still amazes me how well-fed we are compared with other countries. Most clothes are utility now, but they are not too bad. Silk stockings of course are unheard of. By not wearing any stockings during the warmer weather, I find I can manage to stretch out the coupons to get enough for the win-ter.

Needless to say, we were brought up to be fiercely proud of our British heritage. We believed that we were the best country in the world, and we did everything in our power to protect our long history from tyrants like Hitler. We were taught patriotic songs like *Jerusalem, Land of Hope & Glory, There'll Always be an England, and There'll Be Bluebirds over the White Cliffs of Dover.* We clung to our ancient traditions such as singing Christmas carols, dancing around the Maypole every May, Guy Fawkes Day when huge bonfires were lit and men carried barrels of flaming tar through the streets (forbidden during the war), pantomimes, Punch & Judy shows, eating steaming chestnuts at Christmas, Christmas pudding, picnics on the beach, point-to-point horse races, and so on.

Packages from the United States—1943

For us, the Huntleys were magical and mysterious. I never met them, yet their wonderful parcels meant so much and made all the difference to our lives. My mother did not receive any letters from the Huntleys for a while. But then on February 2, 1943, she wrote:

All your packages reached us safely, three food parcels and the very exciting parcel of pyjamas, etc. The children were home from school and they had a glorious time unpacking them. Lots of "Oh! Mummy, just look, lots of lovely things to eat. Can they really buy things in America without 'points'? Points, as you no doubt know, are food coupons. So many have to be surrendered for tinned goods, dried fruits, and tinned milk, etc. I am afraid my little ones know no other way of shopping now. It's rather pathetic really to see them working out how far their sweet coupons will go, especially when I recall the tin that

Jack kept filled with sweets for them. Still, they take it as the only way of living now and they seem very happy and fit. I would like you to know how much we enjoyed the raspberries. I let them have them for tea on Christmas day. The pyjamas were greeted with much enthusiasm. I am trying to find some material the same weight to have them copied so that they will have a change. Fortunately they will be plenty big enough for next year. However they had the joy of parading in them! The dollies are sweet and are named Frances and George!

We managed to get a chicken for Christmas day and I had saved some fruit, mostly supplied by you, so we also had a Christmas pudding and cake made with dried eggs of course. I must tell you, I actually had an egg in a shell a fortnight ago, the first for two months! We are getting used to such notices in the shop windows "shell eggs, allocation No. 1 for registered customers only." So very excitedly I dived in and came out the proud possessor of ONE egg! How I enjoyed it! Milk is also a problem this time of year. I am allowed _ pint every other day. But once a month I can buy a tin of dried milk, equal to a quart of milk. However, we are far from starving and we are all keeping very fit and the children are growing rapidly. I often wonder how Jack would have managed about his appetite if he were with us now. It was a problem when we could buy what we liked.

I still miss him terribly of course, but thoughts of him are always with me and it makes me very sad to know what Tessa and Angela miss. He was such a grand Daddy, lots of fun and knew how to get down to their level. They still speak of him as if he is coming home any moment. They remember him so vividly. It will be two years on April 24 when he sailed away into the unknown. I feel though he is now my guardian angel because everybody is so sweet to me. I have to do a bit of conjuring with the money matters sometimes, but we always seem to just manage. That is one blessing with the rationing; it certainly keeps the housekeeping bills down!

Our countryside is now beginning to look lovely. Beautifully green and the trees are busting into bud. The catkins are out and the crocuses and snowdrops. This part of the country is always first with the spring flowers because the climate is so mild. We have had no winter yet. Today is a real spring day so this afternoon I am going with my friend (her fiancé is also M.N. (Merchant navy) to a place we call the Fire Beacon. It's an old house hidden among the pine trees way up a hill overlooking Sidmouth. It's a grand view and tea is very welcome after the climb.

Mrs. Huntley continued to send parcels and the biggest hit were silk stockings she sent my mother. On June 2, 1943, my mother wrote:

My stockings are the envy of all my friends. I might say they are only worn on very special occasions which, as you may guess, are not very often. There isn't much time for gaiety these days. We have had two dances given for the Canadian boys. They were very jolly. We had lots of Americans too, but I have not yet met anybody from Baltimore. It's always my first question; I'm always hoping they will say Baltimore. I feel I have a special claim on Baltimore.

I have to do fire-guard duty now every eighth night, so it isn't much really. I am exempt when the children are home of course. I am looking forward to them coming home for Whitsun weekend; it's their half-term holiday. They are getting so grownup. Angela has left kindergarten and Tessa is in the third form. She writes and tells me this week that she is starting tennis lessons. How quickly they grow, she will soon want to join a tennis club I suppose! Tessa is her own dear self again, she has at last got over the shock of losing Jack. It's been a slow job, but its so very lovely to see her really laugh and enjoy life again, having lost completely that dreadful reserve she built up which was so unnatural in a child so young. I feel too that I am picking up the threads again and not minding too much.

I see by the newspapers that you have gone on to points, etc. Housekeeping is a work of art, isn't it? It's fruit we miss so much. However our season is coming along and I try to preserve as much as I can and keep for the children when they are home. We were very thrilled about the North African victory. I wonder how much longer? We have been having "Wings for Victory" weeks all over the country and it's amazing the amount of money it has brought in.

I do wish our weather would buck up. It's so cold and wet. The sun is needed so much for the health of the people and our crops.

Our love and grateful thanks to you for all your sweet thoughts.

The next letter my mother wrote was November 18, 1943. She had received no letters since she wrote in June.

I hope you have been receiving my letters. I have not heard from you since you wrote telling me about the loss of your mother. I was so very sorry to have your news because I understand so fully the sense of loss. However, it's amazing how, as time rolls on, that void becomes filled with hundreds of little incidents which do help such a lot. In my own case, since there are no more thoughts of "this time last year, Jack was home etc." I have found it so much easier not to miss him quite so much.

I don't know how to convey to you how thrilled I was with your parcel for the children. I received it about a week ago. The dresses are so very sweet and I know Tessa and Angela will adore them. I am keeping them for Christmas morning. I thank you with all my heart for giving them joy. Anything we have a little out of ordinary (in food especially) the question is always the same "It's from Mrs. Huntley, isn't it Mummy?" You have certainly become their fairy godmother!

We had a great treat a couple of weeks ago: oranges! I saved all the peel and candied it so I will be able to make a Christmas cake, using prunes chopped up instead of currants, and dates and a few sultanas I've saved. Icing sugar is unattainable but we won't let that worry us too much. I am looking forward to the children coming home again in five weeks. It's not much fun keeping house for myself. They are very well and happy and doing well at school. Angela seems to have strong dramatic ability and an amazing memory for poetry, etc., and a good singing voice. Jack would have been so proud to have watched her in the school concert.

*   *   *

The end of the war in Europe certainly seems in sight, don't you think? It's so wonderful to hear our planes cross overhead night after night bent on ending this awful war.

Of course, we looked forward to going home for the holidays but it was strange in a way. We had adjusted to boarding school life and it was the only "family life" we really knew. When we did go home, my mother worked most of the time and went out at night to the pub or with friends and we were left with neighbours. After our father died, our own family life was never the same again. As I have written elsewhere, our best holidays were with our grandparents.

Easter—1944

My mother wrote the following letter to the Huntleys on March 14, 1944.

Tessa and Angela are due home from school in a fortnight's time for the Easter holidays. I look forward to having them home; it's like turning the pages back to the life we once enjoyed. All of us always together, it seems that Jack too comes home then because Angela is growing so like him in her mannerisms and ways of making people laugh.

Tessa is quieter but so very good to me. They of course make a great deal of extra work for me and I'm usually exhausted by the time they return to school. It means running the house, cleaning, cooking, washing, and looking after them as well as still going to business. I leave at 12 noon instead of 1 p.m. to get their lunch and am back again at business at 2.15 p.m. Then I finish at 5 p.m. A friend next door has them at her house while I'm at business. She is very helpful and glad to have them as company for her little boy.

Four years ago, I wouldn't have believed it possible to do so much work and keep well. Shopping I do believe is the greatest problem. I couldn't do it all if Tessa and Angela weren't so helpful. They always lay the table and do the washing up. They also peel the potatoes, make the beds, and clean the silver and brass. Tessa now irons all the handkerchiefs and their underwear. They love doing all these jobs and never have to be asked. I am very lucky, they are so very sweet.

Your parcels came last week. I sent the chocolates to school to Tessa and Angela. I am enclosing the letters they wrote. Tessa is very thrilled with all the Americans stationed at Seaton. She always wants to know if any of them know you. It is so very kind of you to send us all the lovely things. I made a very nice pie with the apple sauce you sent, it was delicious. We are getting oranges again now. About a month ago, we were allowed two lemons each. It came just in time for Pancake Day. I candied the peel of one for next Christmas cake and made a lemon sponge with the other.

Easter—1945

My mother does not seem to have sent any other letters to Mrs. Huntley until March 21, 1945, when she wrote:

We were very thrilled to get your Xmas parcel last week. It's so wonderful to get something to wear without having to give up our precious coupons. We were happy to get your Xmas greetings too and to know that our parcel reached you. Xmas seems a long way back now but I really think it was the nicest we enjoyed since we lost Jack. We had a great big tree which reached the ceiling. Commander Thomas took the children out one day to find it in the woods. Then they had a wonderful time trimming it, they made all the decorations and it really was the most beautiful tree I ever saw. Cmdr. Thomas had dinner with us and the children were delighted to be allowed up for late dinner. He was very happy to be with us. I think everybody likes to feel at home especially at Xmas time. He also came to the pantomime with us "Jack and the Beanstalk." It was the first he had ever seen and he enjoyed it thoroughly. Tessa and Angela were very lucky to be invited to a big party at the US Naval Base. Ice cream almost by the ton and to see our British children enjoy the ice cream was such fun. Lots of the officers were almost in tears because the children were so enjoying themselves. There were about 300 children present.

Tessa and Angela come home tomorrow for the Easter holiday. It will be grand to have them again. They are very fit and happy and doing well at school. The war news is really exciting these days and I feel optimistic about the European war soon being over. We still get the V bombs in London, etc., but here in Sidmouth it's all very peaceful and unwarlike.

Shopping is as difficult as ever, but we are fortunate to get enough even though variety is lacking. At half term I had a treat. Tessa and Angela gave me breakfast in bed, cooked bacon and toast. They were so proud!

Chapter Seven

The End of the War—1945

Germany surrendered on May 7, 1945 and VE (Victory in Europe) Day was declared. I was almost eleven years old. It was a bittersweet day for us, knowing that our father was never coming home again, although my mother continued to cling to the hope that he was "missing" and would miraculously appear some day. I do not remember much about the huge celebrations in the streets, but my mother went to London and told us how exciting it was to be part of the overwhelming joy now that the darkness of war had been lifted. Lights flooded the streets again which fascinated children who had never seen them before.

In spite of the war being over, my mother was in a depressed mood when she wrote to Mrs. Huntley on June 11, 1945.

I was delighted to get your long letter which enabled me to enter into your family circle.

I so look forward to your letters and it would be nicer if time would allow us to exchange news more often. Although the European war is at an end and we now have no blackouts or that fear of raids, etc., life is still so "make-do," shall I call it? I seem to be all the time looking for some stability and it's very difficult to find.

As I sit writing to you, I feel so incomplete. The house is so quiet and empty. I can hear children's voices as they play in the field opposite, but I do not hear Tessa and Angela. They too are away from me. I seem to get so little of them, just the holidays. They are growing up so quickly. Tessa will be eleven in July and Angela eight. They are very fit and happy I know and I do feel very grateful for that. I seem to have come to a full stop. I can't seem to make up my mind what to do. Some days I think I want to give up my job and have the children home and then I feel I would like to move to a different place to live and make new contacts, etc. After all those thoughts I tell myself that I have very good friends here and a comfortable home and the children are having an excellent education, so I'm still here. I suppose everybody feels like that at some time or another, and I for one will be very glad when I get over my unhappy state of mind. I think that we are all very weary of the war and wartime conditions.

You will probably be interested to hear that I was in London for V-day celebrations. I stayed a week. It was very thrilling and seeing the sights took the edge off my losing Jack. We were in Parliament Square when Mr. Churchill made his speech and then we were in a wonderful spot when he drove into the Houses of Parliament. The ovation he got from the crowd brought a lump into my throat. Then later the King, Queen, and Princesses came out onto the balcony of Buckingham Palace. When night came it was a wonderful sight to see the buildings floodlit and huge bonfires flaring up in the parks. I went to a theatre every night, seeing all the best shows that are on just now. And afterwards to dine and dance was just like the old days. It was the first holiday and first time I have been to London since June 1940 when I went with Jack to the American Embassy to arrange for our passage to Boston. You remember we were stopped.

I am hoping so much that traveling will soon buck up and be made easier because I'm longing to meet you all and would like to make the trip over. Only today I had a letter from the children in which they asked how soon they could go to see Frances. You see I had written and told them I had heard from you last week.

Last Tuesday, June 5th, Commander Thomas sailed for the States. We feel very lonely without him. The Naval Base here is closing very soon and he was amongst the first to go. He dined here the night before he went and I feel I have lost a very dear friend. He has promised to call on you and I hope he does because I feel it will cement our present friendship. I know you will be happy to have him look you up and give you all the news.

The country is getting stirred up by our coming election. It's difficult to know who is right and who is wrong. Whoever gets into power will have a hard time trying to get everything straightened out.

I got my new rationing book today. The clothing coupons look very inadequate, especially with two growing daughters. The awful thought is that this system will have to go on for quite a while.

I'm sorry you haven't met Mrs. Thomas yet, but I understand from Trudeau (Cmdr. Thomas) that Carey has been ill practically all winter. Tessa is going up to Guides this summer and Angela is a Brownie. Camping will start again now the war is over.

Japan fought on, but after the Allies dropped atomic bombs, first on Hiroshima, then on Nagasaki, they also surrendered, and August 15 was called VJ (Victory against Japan) Day. The Second World War was finally over. The war had affected civilians as never before, and children perhaps most of all. Millions of British children had been evacuated their education disrupted, and their lives turned upside down by the absence of fathers.

For many of them, nightmares and nervous problems haunted them for years. In my case, World War II left me with a virulent hatred of war and a keen awareness of its futility.

The British royal family, King George V1, Queen Elizabeth, and the two Princesses Elizabeth and Margaret stayed in London throughout the war, even though Buckingham Palace was bombed. They were a great source of comfort to the British people and showed unusual courage and bravery by suffering through the blitz along with them. King George gave a certificate to all school children in June 1946 as part of the first anniversary celebrating the end of the war. It said:

Today we celebrate victory; I send this personal message to you and all other boys and girls at school. For you have shared in the hardships and dangers of a total war and you have shared no less in the triumph of the Allied Nations. I know you will always feel proud to belong to a country which was capable of such supreme effort; proud, too, of parents and elder brothers and sisters who by their courage, endurance, and enterprise brought victory. May these qualities be yours as you grow up and join in the common effort to establish among the nations of the world unity and peace.

Signed, George R.I.

For my sister and me, the end of the war meant leaving boarding school and returning home. Unbeknownst to us, a whole new life lay ahead of us, and once again we would be on the move.

Back Home—1946–1947

English Girl,

German Boy

When we arrived back in Sidmouth, my mother enrolled us in the Convent of the Assumption, an elite private school for girls who came from all over the world. Although it was Catholic, most of the students came from other religions. I only spent two years there, but it had a profound effect on my life. Up until the age of 12, I did not belong to any religious faith, but had experienced the Baptist and Anglican beliefs through my grandparents and boarding school. I had never even been baptized.

I loved the ritual of the Catholic Church in those days: the drama of the Mass, the colourful vestments worn by the priests, daily Benediction services when we donned white veils, the clouds of smoking incense hanging in the air. For me, it was like the theatre! In those days, nuns were covered from head to toe in heavy robes and white habits. We had to curtsey to them whenever we passed them in corridors and stand when they entered the classroom. When we did well in school, we won ribbons with religious medals which we hung proudly around our necks. We had two houses— St. Peter's and St. Paul's—which we joined when we had achieved high academic standing, sports perform- ance, and good conduct. The houses competed against each other, and I was so proud when I was asked to join St. Peter's and could pin a red badge on my uni- form. St. Paul's had green badges. We also exchanged holy pictures and wrote messages on them to special friends—I still have some today which I received when I left for Canada.

I was baptized a Catholic in May 1947, a momentous turning point in my life. I received many holy pictures from friends and teachers alike, congratulating me on being received into the Church. I even received a holy picture from Mother Helen, the Mother Superior, "in memory of learning to answer Mass." The mass was entirely in Latin, so it was quite an effort and accomplishment. To become a Catholic, I had to adopt a saint's name, so I took the name Teresa after Saint Teresa, the nearest I could get to Tessa.

Chapter Eight

War Brides

War brides were the young women who met, fell in love with, and married Canadian and American servicemen in the Second World War. Forty-eight thousand women from Britain, along with 22,000 children, followed their husbands to Canada during and after the war. Canadian servicemen stationed in Britain during World War II spent a great deal of time waiting to be assigned to the European theatre. Boredom set in, so they spent time visiting local canteens and service clubs where they met local young women, some still in their teens. They were mostly shop girls and those working in various capacities for the government. Romances blossomed and, because nobody knew how much time they had, whirlwind weddings took place in short order. Many hardly knew each other, and husbands soon left for battle not knowing their wives were pregnant. Babies were born and not seen by their fathers for years, and sometimes never. Wives became single parents trying to cope with new motherhood when they'd scarcely had time to enjoy married life.

When the war ended in 1945, it was time to bring these families together. Canadian servicemen had married women from Britain, the Netherlands, France, Germany, Belgium, Norway, Sweden, and Italy. Often, with only a few hours' notice, the war brides packed what they could and said good-bye to parents they may never see again. Like pioneering women before them, they sailed in camouflaged ships with little knowledge of their future country or husbands. Most of them made the crossing in 1946 aboard such ships as the Queen Mary, the Ile de France, the Scythia, and the Aquitania, leaving from Southampton. Their journey across the ocean was uncomfortable as they were jammed into crowded sleeping quarters on lower decks, and many suffered from seasickness.

Canadian war brides arrived in Halifax at Pier 21 and from there were scattered all across Canada. Nothing could have prepared them for what lay ahead. City-born women found themselves on farms in remote communities; some were not welcomed by their new relations or by communities who disliked their "foreign-ness." Some of their husbands died before they'd been in Canada for a year. Some were beaten, others abandoned, some couldn't wait to get back to England, and others never wanted to return. However, many of the war brides have celebrated 60 years of wedded life and have contributed greatly to Canadian life. In 2000, a memorial plaque was mounted at Pier 21 in honour of the contribution they have made to Canada.

My mother always became very indignant and bristled at the suggestion that she too was a war bride. She felt she was a cut above because she married an officer and did not belong to the "shop girl" class. It seems most of the war brides married ordinary ranks and not officers. Indeed, perhaps she was right, since she married her Canadian husband after the war in Canada and not during the war in England. She met Major Frederick Carroll Manley at the Bowd Inn in Sidmouth when he was on leave enjoying some rest and relaxation. Periodically, officers took some time off and Sidmouth was a magnet for many of them. My mother had been a widow for three years and was a chemist at Boot's the Chemist. She was an attractive 33 year-old widow with two young children, and was beginning to enjoy life again after the tragic loss of my father.

Major Fred Manley

Major Frederick Carroll Manley was the complete opposite of my father both in looks and personality. He was very good-looking with sandy-blond hair and blue eyes, and had managed to escape marriage until he was forty. In pre-war Montreal, Freddie was a much sought-after bachelor, the darling of debutante society who could have married into any of Montreal's top Irish Catholic families. In particular, the five daughters of one-time mayor Sir William Hingston and Lady Hingston were especially keen, but to no avail. They went on to marry others, but remained good friends, and he was godfather to some of their children. His own godfather was John Carroll, a lieutenant governor of Quebec from whom he got his middle name, Carroll.

Fred was a quiet, extremely kind man who never said a bad word about anybody. We could not have asked for a better stepfather. A talented athlete, he excelled at every sport he tried, especially rugby, lacrosse, and golf. He was an active member of the Montreal Amateur Athletic Association, playing on the club's lacrosse team. He played on champion rugby teams for Loyola College and McGill University. He graduated from McGill University with a law degree, but never practised law. Apparently, he never really worked until he joined the army, but spent much of his time traveling with his mother, May McGuirk.

Fred's father, also Frederick, was born in Brockville, Ontario. He was president of Dominion Trust but died at 38 of uremia. Descended from Empire Loyalists, one of his ancestors was Sir John O'Donnell. He was very handsome, a wonderful pianist, and wealthy. He and May had another child, Evelyn, who died at the age of 15 of a thyroid condition. After Evelyn died, they separated. The stock market crash of 1929 wiped out most of his wealth, but he did eventually make some of it back. They were one of the first families to own a car in Montreal, a Pierce Arrow. May McGuirk came from Irish stock—her father was William McGuirk who travelled the world importing linens and silks. She had a special trunk with all kinds of remnants of materials he had bought. She had a sister Eva who never married.

May Manley,
Tessa's step-grandmother,
late 1800s.

Aunt May never married again after she and Frederick separated, but, according to my mother, had a long-standing affair with a prominent Montreal politician after whom a famous boulevard is named. She had a suite in the Windsor Hotel and openly rode with him in his carriage. He gave her many gifts, including some jewelry that we still have today. Aunt May (she did not like the idea of being a grandmother!)was also a founding member of the Montreal Museum of Fine Arts and played an active role in the art world. The Manleys were in the upper echelon of the Montreal Irish Catholic community and counted many of the leading politicians of the time as friends. Fred boarded at Loyola College and used to tell stories of visiting his mother at the Windsor Hotel and roller skating around the corridors!

Fred was second in command of his regiment (The Royal Rifles of Canada) and stationed in Camberley, England. He was responsible for the movement of troops back and forth across the English Channel in preparation for the big push to end the war. His movements were all very hush-hush. My mother never knew when he was coming to visit; he would suddenly appear. Nor did she receive any letters because of security concerns. But our family did receive a huge Christmas parcel from his mother in Canada containing food we had not seen in the war years: ham, butter, bacon, sugar, candies, cookies, and nylon stockings. In 1945, Fred suddenly appeared in Sidmouth to say he was being shipped back to Canada and to propose to my mother. My mother accepted, and "Uncle Fred" returned to Canada to prepare to marry my mother and inherit two children at the same time! It had been a strange sort of whirlwind courtship.

I had very mixed feelings about having a stepfather, leaving England and my school. We had been without a father for seven years, and I felt we had done perfectly well without one. In addition, nobody could replace my father. To top it all, I was entering the difficult years of adolescence. My sister, three years younger than me, adored Uncle Fred and was clearly delighted with having a father to replace the one she had never really known. Of course, the prospect of going to a new country was very exciting. Uncle Fred told us stories of ice palaces, cowboys and Indians, and igloos; any child would be excited at the prospect of experiencing so many new things. But I loved my school and did not want to leave, and my mother even suggested I stay in boarding school in England. I felt torn, but curiosity about my new life got the better of me, and I decided on Canada for better or worse.

Chapter Nine

Leaving for Canada—1947

There does not seem to have been much correspondence with Mrs. Huntley until January 26, 1947. My sister Angela and I enclosed thank you letters and photos with this letter from my mother. In my letter, I said I loved my school and did not want to leave it.

Dear Mrs. Huntley,

We were all so happy to hear from you again. We love your letters telling us all your news of the family. Yesterday your parcels arrived and were unpacked with much excitement. The children loved the purses and chocolates and, as for me, the dresses are a godsend and fit me perfectly and are just the right colours. They mean such a saving in coupons. I feel I must keep our coupons for warm clothing.

While I write, Tessa and Angela are going through their dance number. They attend a dancing school and have been chosen for a duet dance. Angela is taking the part of the girl and Tessa the boy. They are very pleased as it is their first dance in public. The school is giving a display and it's a great moment for Angela. It's her first dance up on points and to use her words "a real, true ballet dress Mummy." As you say, little girls are so interesting.

Thank you so much for your good wishes and understanding. I'm sure we will be very happy and when we meet in the not too distant future, I feel sure you will like Fred very much. I'm still waiting for my landing letter—these formalities are very wearisome and slow. The number of forms I've collected already would paper a room. I am however making progress and fortunately helped by many friends.

We have had snow today and it's quite a job to keep warm. Gas pressure is reduced and cuts made in the electricity and I'm allowed a small ration of coal per week. Life is really much harder than it seemed during the war. Food is so monotonous and very little of it.

Bacon has been cut to 2 oz. a week which we are allowed to collect each fortnight. Our rations this week for the three of us amounted to the grand total of 3 shillings and nine pence!! Marmalade, scrubbing soap, or toilet soap just haven't been available for eight weeks and it's four weeks since we have had an egg. Then we are told that things are not very bright for the future! I am luckier than most, Fred sends a parcel each month which definitely helps to make meals more interesting.

What type of clothing do you think I should try and get to take to Canada? We are hoping to go in May. I understand I will be granted 50 extra coupons, enough to make me dance with joy to see that number.

I was pleased to hear you liked our small Kmas gift. I thought the book might interest you both. It's Angela's bedtime, so I'll have to stop now and see her off. It's nice to hear Frances is doing well with her piano lessons; it gives such pleasure to her and others.

I will certainly let you know my address, but before that will inform you of my sailing date etc.

Shortly after Fred returned to Canada, he joined the company of his good friend Harold McNamara who had a contract to build the Laurentian highway north of Quebec City. We had to wait 18 months before we could leave England because there was no transporta-

English
Girl,

German
Boy

tion and there were still mines in the English Channel. In June 1947, the Atlantic Ocean was declared safe and mine-free for passenger ships to cross. We embarked in Southampton and, unlike the war brides before us, travelled first class on the SS Aquitania which had been a troopship during the war. We packed very few belongings, the most precious of which were our bicycles. My mother was seasick for the entire crossing, so we were left to our own devices and passed the time with the returning troops. It took us seven days until we finally saw land and our first glimpse of Canada.

We sailed into Halifax on July 1, 1947, not realizing it was Dominion Day (Canada Day), Canada's national holiday. Fleets of small sailboats greeted us, horns were blowing—we thought it was a special welcome for us! The first thing that struck my mother was the sky; she had never seen such a high sky. We then took a train to Montreal. We went first class, and I remember not being able to open the window as we could on English trains. It seemed strange to us that all the people working on the train were black. The train had a nice dining parlour with white tablecloths and waiters who wore white gloves. It was the first time we had ever slept on a train. We arrived at Windsor Station in Montreal at 7:30 in the morning, dressed in our tweed suits in the heat of a Canadian summer. Fred and his mother, Aunt May, were waiting for us. Fred introduced us to her, and she put her arms around my mother and said "what a brave little girl you are!" We had a wonderful reunion.

My mother married Fred in St. Patrick's Cathedral, Montreal, Canada on July 9, 1947. He was a wonderful husband, father, and grandfather for 31 years.

She wrote an account of her first Christmas in Canada and described her impressions of *A Christmas I'll Never Forget* as follows:

A crisp, clear night gliding through the deep snow in a sleigh on our way to Midnight Mass— my first Christmas in Canada! It was 1947. We had been invited to spend Christmas Eve with the Villeneuve family who lived in Stoneham, 14 miles north of Quebec City. This family of eleven children had adopted us, my two little girls, and my new Canadian husband when we arrived in Canada to make our life together. My previous husband, a merchant navy officer had been lost at sea during the Battle of the Atlantic in 1941. Mrs. Villeneuve was a wonderful neighbour. In spite of being four miles apart, she found time to teach me how to quilt, how to shop for the right winter clothing, and how to shop for food. After the austerity of rationing and coupons for clothing in wartime Britain, it was overwhelming to find such an abundance of everything available to us. Her children taught mine how to skate and ski and, in the summertime, to fish and all the ways of a good new world. Most of all she taught me how to tame the iron wood stove.

Peggy and Fred Manley on their wedding day, July 8, 1947. Montreal, Quebec.

English
Girl,

German
Boy

I learnt how to bake and cook on it and how to keep it going supplied by an enormous wood pile. The stove had to heat the house during winter and it was quite an art keeping it fed throughout the night. Christmas Eve was like a scene out of fairyland. The church and houses were sparkling with lights and the church bell rang calling us to mass. All the sleighs arrived from the surrounding villages and everybody shouted greetings to friends. All the brightly coloured coats and jackets made the snow seem even whiter.

The church was decked with evergreens and Christmas trees trimmed with miniature lights at the altar and the nativity scene was made by the school children. The mass was a joyous one and afterwards we returned to the Villeneuve home for the "Reveillon," the traditional Christmas Eve feast celebrated by French Quebecers.

The littlest child came down the stairs in his sleeping suit and joined in. The table was laden with ham, tourtiere pies (a must in a French-Canadian home), salads, breads, Christmas cake, minced meat pies, and sherry to toast each other. Even the children each had a glass! The happy, surprised faces of the children were a delight as they eagerly opened their presents. How can I ever forget the privilege of being part of that wonderful family as they shared their home and their love with us newcomers?

My Mother's Life in Canada

My mother's life radically changed when she moved to Quebec from England in July 1947. She found herself in the small village of Notre Dame des Laurentides, north of Quebec City, with French-Canadians as neighbours. She spoke no French and they spoke no English, so it was a difficult and lonely life at first. She had to feed a wood stove night and day to keep warm and to do all her cooking. Her new husband was often away supervising the building of the Laurentian highway, and we children were gone all day to school in Quebec City. Her closest neighbour was an old French-Canadian trapper who helped her in emergencies. It was certainly not the life she had expected.

At the time, Maurice Duplessis was Premier and his reign was called le grand noiceur (the great darkness). He kept a tight fist over Quebecers, urging them to have more babies, to enter the priesthood, the law, or education, but definitely not the world of commerce. It was common to see families with 10 or more children, and the churches were packed on Sundays. In those days, it was unthinkable not to wear a hat or veil, stockings and gloves. Everyone wore their Sunday best; short skirts, jeans, shorts, and sleeveless dresses were out of the question. Contrast that with today, when many Quebecers do not go to church and are choosing neither to marry nor to have children—Quebec currently has the lowest birth rate in Canada.

We moved to Quebec City after awhile, and my stepfather rejoined the army and worked at the Valcartier base. Life changed considerably. In 1947, the population of Quebec had a 15% English-speaking minority. There were three distinct communities: French-Canadians, Irish Catholics, and English Protestants. French-Canadians and Irish Catholics frequently intermarried. At the top end of the social scale, the French and English mingled socially with ease. My mother and Fred quickly settled into this group through their political friends who included them in all their social functions. In turn, my mother did her fair share of entertaining diplomats and other well-known politicians such as the St. Laurents and the Lesages.

My mother joined the IODE (Imperial Order Daughters of the Empire) and eventually became Regent (President). They raised a good deal of money every year by staging *The Gaieties*, a highly popular song and dance production. With her musical and theatrical background, she was a bright light and thoroughly enjoyed her role. Eventually, she moved to Ste. Petronille, Island of Orleans where she and Fred had a wonderful time renovating an old French farmhouse and planting a rock garden which attracted visitors from all over the world. My mother helped organize summer concerts on the Island and, according to her, the famous French-Canadian singer, Gilles Vigneault, wrote his record-breaking song *Mon Pays* in their house!

There are no more letters from the Huntleys until June 1955. By this time, we had been in Canada for 8 years. In her final letter, my mother writes from Ste. Petronille, Island of Orleans, Quebec.

Dear Mrs. Huntley,

I was delighted to get the announcement of Frances' graduation. You must be very proud of her; it's such an exciting time and a feeling of accomplishment. I do hope she will go along happily and successfully in her choice of career. Angela has another year, having lost a year by attending French convent to get her French. We are without Tessa since May 18th. She has gone to England for an indefinite time. She is visiting about 4 months Jack's people and mine and then she plans to work. Maybe by then she will want to come home.

Jack's sisters are visiting me for a month arriving July 9. I went back in February and stayed until May. I wasn't recovering too well from an operation last August. I'm grand now and it was so nice to see my mother and all my friends. I wish you could bring Frances to see us this *summer. I would like you to meet Jack's sisters; you think it over and let me know.*

Write me and tell me about the graduation, what Frances wears etc., Angela is so interested to know. By her photograph, she looks such a lovely girl. I will be looking for a letter.

When Fred was in his early 50's, both his mother and aunt died, leaving him enough money so he could comfortably retire. My mother and he wanted to escape the severe Quebec winters, and so spent six months of the year in Clearwater Beach, Florida. They sold their Island of Orleans property and moved to Ottawa. Fred had been a two-pack-a-day smoker and it finally caught up with him. Sadly, in 1978 he died of lung cancer and cancer of the liver at the Veteran's Hospital. He was a prince of a man and a wonderful stepfather and grandfather. An extraordinary thing happened as he lay dying surrounded by our family. His face became young again, his eyes lit up and he reached out to the orderly standing by his bed and mouthed the name "Martin." Our eldest child, Martin, had died tragically three years earlier, and it seemed that Fred was reaching out to him as he passed from this world to the next. It was such a vivid experience and stays with all of us today.

After Fred's death, my mother moved to Oakville, Ontario to be closer to us, but still spent winters in Florida. She married a third time to Dr. Stanley Brown, a Canadian from the Eastern Townships in Quebec. Unfortunately, the marriage did not last and she divorced him after four years. She was still attractive well into her 80s and seemed to always have male friends. When we moved to Costa Rica, she decided she wanted to die in England and so moved there in 1996 and lived with my sister. However, it was not for long. She had only been there three months when she suffered a stroke and died at the age of 87. She had been plagued by heart problems in her later years, the result of an episode of rheumatic fever she suffered as a child.

My mother found the seven years after Fred died of cancer the most difficult. She suffered many losses of loved ones: her two brothers, her husband Jack, her father and mother, her grandson Martin, and numerous close friends. My mother found the loss of my son very difficult because it was a double sorrow: she also grieved and suffered for me, her daughter. In my mother's words, we did all rise from the ashes of despair, eventually.

Chapter Ten

My Life in Canada

I celebrated my 13th birthday on July 12, twelve days after we arrived in Canada. Thirteen is probably the most difficult age to change countries and fathers. After the initial awe of seeing so many big cars, tall buildings, wide streets, and full grocery stores, reality quickly set in. Going to a new school was the worst part. Up until then, I had always gone to posh private schools. Now I found myself in a public Irish Catholic high school in Quebec City, run by nuns belonging to the Sisters of Charity. I skipped Grade 8 and was bumped up to Grade 9 because the education in England was more advanced. There were no uniforms, and I was in class with 15-year-olds who wore makeup and nylon stockings. I, on the other hand, still wore kilts and knee socks and my hair was in pigtails. I felt totally out of place. Everyone mocked my strong British accent, which made me all the more determined to hang on to it. I plunged into my school work and was soon at the top of the class, excelling in Latin, history, religion, and English literature. I had no trouble with French since I had learned it starting in Form 1 in England. I gradually made good friends who were equally academic. We had two educational streams, classical and commercial. I chose classical because I wanted to go on to university rather than spend my life as a secretary.

I had little interest in boys, and dreaded going to dances where the boys stood on one side of the room and girls on the other. My friends and I were generally taller than the boys, so we were not asked to dance very often. I hated Canada and longed to go back to

England, and it became my goal to leave as soon as I could. My unhappiness led to allergies of all sorts. I had a battery of tests showing I was allergic to most foods and many other things. I began suffering from dreadful migraine headaches and brain tumours were suspected, but after extensive tests, none were found. Everybody concluded the symptoms were related to my emotional state. So I escaped into my own world and wrote poetry and short stories and listened to classical music.

Our musical education at school was outstanding. Dr. Wilfrid Pelletier, a well-known orchestra conductor, offered a series of concerts for high school students to educate us about the great composers, the function of all the musical instruments in the orchestra, and to instill in us a love of classical music. I owe my love of music to Dr. Pelletier, his concerts were so enriching and inspiring. Salle Wilfrid Pelletier at Place des Arts in Montreal is named after him.

English Girl, German Boy

First Job—1950

After I graduated from high school in 1950 at the age of 16, I landed a summer job as a reporter for the Quebec Chronicle-Telegraph, North America's oldest English language daily and one of newspaper magnate Roy Thomson's first acquisitions. I was supposed to go to university in the fall, but I loved the job so much I stayed on for a year. The Women's Editor had just left, so I took on that job and had to prepare four pages each day. I covered fashion shows, social events, Princess Elizabeth's royal tour, criminal cases at the court house, and Maurice Duplessis' press conferences which were more like sermons—nobody dared challenge him. I also interviewed famous people like movie star Montgomery Clift and pianist Arthur Rubinstein. It was all very exciting for a 16-year-old and was also a big responsibility.

My co-workers were all hard-bitten newsmen much older than me. They sipped away at flasks of whisky which stood on their desks. Clouds of cigarette smoke filled one large room where we all sat banging away on old typewriters. My four pages had to be "put to bed" before I left for the day and the proofs checked carefully for any errors. In those days, newspapers were typeset on lead bars so if a change needed to be made, I had to find the appropriate lead bar and change it. It was quite a messy business.

In the 1950s, women were expected to go into nursing, teaching, secretarial work, or go to university to find a husband. My mother thought that being a journalist was not a "real job" and that I should do something more meaningful. She suggested nursing, given her own background as a chemist. I reluctantly left the newspaper and was accepted as a "probie" at the old Montreal General Hospital in the east end of Montreal near St. Lawrence Blvd., then known as the ghetto. "Probie" was short for a probation of six months to see whether or not nursing was for you. After six months, "probies" were capped. It took three more years until graduation. Our uniform was a dress with pink and white stripes and stiff white aprons, white stockings, and white oxford shoes. We lived in residence at the hospital, and when we went outside we wore navy blue capes to show we were not women of "bad reputation," since at that time St. Lawrence Blvd. was home to prostitutes and down-and-outs.

We had to be on the wards at 7 a.m. to empty bed pans, bath patients, give them back rubs, serve meals, and make beds, and then go to class for the rest of the day. We then had to go on the wards again at 7 p.m. to clean up the patients. Worst of all, we had to do night shifts as well. I worked on both the surgical and medical wards. I really did not like the medical wards which were filled with cancer patients, diabetics, and patients with various other diseases. I remember how devastated I was when one of my favourite patients, an old Polish diabetic who had gangrene and had lost his leg, died while I was attending him. That was when I decided nursing was not for me. I was only there three months. I loved the academic part, but hated the actual nursing. The head nurse, Miss Mackenzie, begged me to stay, saying that I would be an excellent nurse.

Meeting Martin

When I left nursing, I worked for a brief time at the Montreal Gazette newspaper. I made friends with Louise Chevalier whose boyfriend Gunther was Austrian. One day she asked me to go with her to one of Montreal's popular coffee houses where she was going to meet him. Gunther's friend, Martin Börner (known as Eddie), was also there. He was 23, good-looking, and seemed very suave and worldly to an 18-year-old girl who had never had a serious relationship. I suppose it was love at first sight, but our romance only lasted a month because I was not prepared to "go all the way." I returned to Quebec City and was very unhappy when I learned he had a new girlfriend almost right away.

I needed to earn money so I could reach my dream of going back to England. I went to business school for a year and learned shorthand, typing, and bookkeeping. I landed a job in the secretarial pool at Anglo-Canadian Pulp & Paper in Quebec City, saved up $500, and sailed to England on the "Samaria" in 1955.

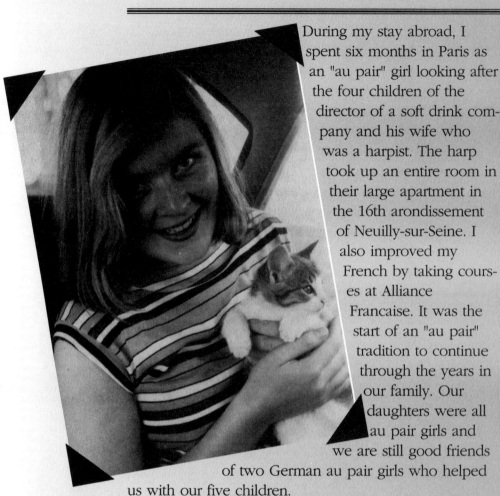

During my stay abroad, I spent six months in Paris as an "au pair" girl looking after the four children of the director of a soft drink company and his wife who was a harpist. The harp took up an entire room in their large apartment in the 16th arondissement of Neuilly-sur-Seine. I also improved my French by taking courses at Alliance Francaise. It was the start of an "au pair" tradition to continue through the years in our family. Our daughters were all au pair girls and we are still good friends of two German au pair girls who helped us with our five children.

Photo of Tessa taken by Martin soon after they first met in Montreal in 1957.

I then worked as a journalist for a magazine for two years, and worked as an usherette at the National Film Theatre at night. I only earned 9 pounds a week working both jobs, enough to pay for a bed sit in South Kensington. I fell in love with an Italian graphic artist who worked at the British Broadcasting Corporation (BBC). We became engaged, but I had promised my parents I would return to Canada for a short visit after I had been away for two years. I set sail again in April 1957, tearfully saying good-bye to Carlo and promising to return soon.

When I returned to Canada, I went to Montreal to look up some mutual friends of Martin's. They suggested I call him to say I was back. We met again and spent a weekend with friends in the Laurentians where he asked me to marry him. It was a real dilemma—I was engaged to someone else and wanted to return to England. Carlo was Catholic, so was I, but Martin was Lutheran, a problem in those days because a Catholic could not marry a Protestant in a Catholic church; the Protestant had to take "instruction" and promise to bring up children as Catholics. In the end, fate decided for me.

Martin in 1953, two years after arriving in Montreal.

Wedding—1957

On August 3, 1957, Martin and I married in the sacristy of the little church in Ste. Petronille, Island of Orleans. We brought up five children in Montreal. My entire British family, fiercely anti-German, was against the marriage. Martin's parents, on the other hand, expressed no such hostility toward me. When I first met Martin, he said he was Swiss due to the prevailing postwar prejudice toward Germans. I was determined to

bring up our children to be proud of their German heritage, and insisted they learn German, work in Germany, and learn about both sides of World War II. We accomplished this in spite of lingering anti-German prejudice that existed in the 1950s, 1960s, and even today. Nevertheless, we persisted, and our children are the richer for it.

World War II greatly influenced my life. In fact, if there had been no war, I probably would not have worked at all. My father, if he had lived, would have sent me to a fine school in Switzerland and then marriage. But I think the war made me a stronger and more independent person, and I learned leadership and discipline during my six years in boarding school.

Tessa and Martin on their wedding day, August 3, 1957. Ste. Petronille, Island of Orleans, Quebec.

The destruction of German cities by allied bombing with civilians as targets vastly outnumbered the damage done to English cities by German bombers. It is a known fact that Winston Churchill, "hero" Bomber Arthur Harris, and others deliberately laid waste German cities and killed over 600,000 innocent civilians to demoralize the population to bring the war to an end. There are not many first-hand accounts of the Dresden holocaust, and we hope Martin's story will contribute to a better understanding of what it was like to survive that dreadful inferno. The sad part is that not one single member of the British and United States allied command was ever held accountable in a court of law for the deliberate massacre of so many innocent people.

The role the Russians played in WWII as allies of the British and Americans is often overlooked. During the 60th anniversary commemorations in 2005, they were often portrayed as heroic liberators when, in fact, they sent one million Poles in trainloads to the death camps in Siberia. They rampaged and raped their way through East Germany, where no woman or girl was safe. They turned East Germany into one large prison from which there was no escape, and created concentration camps of their own for people who did not tow the party line—they believed this is what the German people deserved. On the other hand, the West Germans benefited from the Marshall Plan and never looked back. There was no such help for the East Germans, only 44 years of misery and hopelessness.

English girl,

German Boy

Martin, aged 17, the eldest child of
Tessa and Martin.
This photo was taken a week before his
tragic death in a mountaineering accident
in Switzerland, May 3, 1975.

Tessa and Martin with their
five children. Montreal, 1972.
Martin is holding Jason,
Hilary standing. Martin seated.
In the front row, Heidi (holding our
dachshund Putzi), Megan, and Tessa.

Part Two-German Boy
Martin's Story

Martin and his sister Elfriede in 1934.

Chapter Eleven

Family History

The rolling hills and the steep valleys were covered with a dense, dark forest. An abundance of deer, wolves, and bear roamed under the canopies of spruce, pine, and majestic beach trees. The clear mountain brooks were filled with trout. This is the first recorded description of the Erzgebirge, the Ore Mountains, the east-west mountain range separating the present Czech Republic from Saxony, in the former East Germany.

History books tell us that the roots of European civilizations are found in Mesopotamia, the present Iraq. From there, Indo-Germanic tribes moved north, bringing with them their culture, intelligence, and knowledge of melting ore into metals from which they forged tools and weapons. The indigenous Neanderthal inhabitants of Europe could not compete with these tribes and vanished.

Two thousand years before Christ, central Europe was populated by Celtic tribes. They had to yield to the pressure of the Slavs from the east and the Germanic tribes from the north. Their remnants are now found in Wales, Ireland, and Scotland. From then to the time of the birth of Christ, the movement of the tribes in Europe intensified. Some Angles and Saxons moved to present day England; a cockney from London can still understand the Low German dialect spoken in Hamburg. Other Saxons moved south to the present Saxony. The Goths and Vikings from Denmark and Sweden moved east to the Ukraine, while the Slavs and Sorbs moved west to the south-eastern part of central Europe.

English Girl, German Boy

These movements and the great influence of the Roman Empire created the roads and passes over the mountains for armies and trade. One of these roads leads from the area of Dresden to Dohna, Kulm, Teplice, and Prague, which was a very early centre of European culture. Traders who travelled the road from Dresden to Prague over the inhospitable mountain pass of the Erzgebirge told of the rough climate and of robbers hiding in the dark forests. This pass is about 20 kilometers from Hirschsprung (the valley of the jumping deer) near Altenberg, the place of my birth in 1929.

My Mother's Family

I found the earliest member of my family tree in Zittau near Bautzen, in the wedge of Germany between Poland and the Czech Republic. Ludwig Buttig lived around 1480. He was a pond guard, an important position in which he was responsible for collecting and storing water year-round. The water was used for driving the water wheels that provided energy for the looms of the cloth weavers for which Zittau was famous. Zittau was a stopover for the caravans bringing silks, spices, and bronze from the east to Prague. It was a wealthy town and was ransacked many times by the armies of feuding kings.

Zittau also had a small area of about three square kilometers with particularly rich dark soil and a climate much milder than its immediate surroundings. In this soil, the first fresh vegetables grew after the long winters. The first lettuce was particularly in strong demand. The farmers' daughters from this tiny bit of land were referred to as "Salad Princesses," and my grandmother was one of them. She told my mother how, in about 1870, she helped her father load a horse-drawn wagon full of lettuce, and she described the overnight drive to Dresden to sell the lettuce at the market. It sold quickly and for a good price—these were the first fresh greens after a long winter. This princess was not only beautiful but also intelligent, and she came with a dowry. My grandfather knew a good thing when he saw it, and proposed. He was a tall handsome man and was readily accepted. They had seven children; my mother was the youngest, born in 1888.

My grandfather, Clemens Schenk came from a family of cloth weavers, but he preferred to operate restaurants and hotels. His last hotel was in Schmiedeberg, Erzgebirge, halfway between Dresden and the hunting castle of the Saxon Kings in Rehefeld in the mountains, four kilometers from my birthplace. The royal family frequently stopped over at my grandfather Schenk's hotel for a rest. One time, the princesses were sitting in the open carriage having just eaten fresh doughnuts. They held up their sticky fingers, not knowing what to do with them and the King, a down-to-earth type, told them "why don't you just lick your paws!" My mother laughed, but not openly! This

Martin's maternal grandparents Maria Emma Buttig and Clemens Schenk, born circa 1850 in Saxony, Germany.
She was the "salad princess" and he owned hotels.

era of kings and castles came to an abrupt end in 1914 with the start of World War I.

My Father's Family

For hundreds of years, the Börner family were farmers in the flat and fertile lands along the Elbe River. When his father died in 1776, Gottlieb Börner was paid his share of the inheritance, hitched up a team of horses, loaded his wife, children, and worldly goods on a wagon, and rolled into the foothills of the Erzgebirge to St. Michaelis, near Freiberg. He bought a farm there, where his descendants live to this day. Freiberg and its surrounding villages had been a going concern ever since silver was discovered there in about 1100. Gottlieb thought that with a good mining industry nearby and fertile land for farming, the future of his family would be secure. And it was. The mines were very productive and its mining technology led the world. Today, the Mining University of Freiberg still attracts many international students.

Around 1400, tin ore was found in Altenberg, 50 km to the east, and soon a mining town of 73 houses was built. In 1883, my grandfather Carl Börner bought a small hotel and restaurant in Altenberg, following his ancestor's experience: where there is mining, there is business. In those days, after a three-year apprenticeship, young boys wandered to other towns and countries to work in their trade to further improve their skills. When these wanderers stopped at my grandfather's inn for a beer and food, they told tales about their experiences in other lands. Not all were true, but all were interesting. In 1896, when he was six years old, my grandmother told my father to "come, sit on a little footstool under the table, and listen to what this wanderer has to tell!" This story-telling was the main source of information.

In 1908, my grandfather was asked to collect the share of his inheritance from the family farm. He and my father walked for two days from Altenberg to St. Michaelis along the windblown ridge of the Ore Mountains. My father told me how heavy the sacks of gold coins were that they had to carry home on their shoulders, and how often they had to rest. With this inheritance, my grandfather built Buschhaus, a guest house and country inn in Hirschsprung, where I was born in 1929.

When researching my family's history over the past 500 years, three things stood out:

- My male ancestors usually married two or three times because their wives died in childbirth. This stopped only after Louis Pasteur discovered sepsis, around 1860.
- My ancestors were survivors. They survived the Black Death and endless wars. In the 17th century, two-thirds of the population of central Europe perished in religious wars, famines, and disease.
- In 500 years, the little mining town of Altenberg was destroyed five times through wars, the last time in 1945.

My Father, Martin

Hotel Schmiedeberg, early 1900's, owned by Martin's grandfather, Clemens Schenk. It was the favourite stopover for the kings of Saxony on their way to their hunting castle in the mountains.

In 1914, at age 24, my father was drafted into the army of the Kaiser. He was a telephone linesman, connecting the front lines to the command posts in the rear. He served in the Alsace-Lorraine in France, and also in Serbia. When he came home in 1918, the country was in shambles. With the Treaty of Versailles, the victorious Allies wanted to make sure that Germany would never get on its feet again. The results were catastrophic. There was starvation for three years, followed by hyperinflation for another three years which wiped out any savings. Then a new currency was introduced which was based on gold. It was a good idea for stability, but nobody had any money, and there was very little money in circulation. There were no jobs, as industry was shackled by the Treaty of Versailles.

Germany had produced the world's leading composers, poets, philosophers, scientists, engineers, architects, and artists, and now it was being kept down in despair and hopelessness. Then came the stock market crash in 1929, which added to the existing problems. Is it any wonder that a demagogue like Adolf Hitler got hold of the minds of the people in 1933 by promising work, pride, and a better future?

The currency quickly changed, its value based on German work, not gold. Roads were built, industries grew, exports started up, there was food and pride. Along with this, there was a buildup of armed forces. Within three years, the 1936 Olympic Games in Berlin were a great success, but they were also used as a great propaganda tool. In 1937, my father had enough confidence to expand our inn by adding a verandah restaurant seating 60 guests. But then political tensions grew with the marches into Austria, Sudetenland, and the Saarland. In 1939, only six years after Hitler's takeover, Germany had the most modern army in the world. World War II started, and it ended six years later in 1945 with the almost total destruction of Germany. My father next lived under Russian occupation, and until his death in 1973, he lived in the East German Republic, under Communism. None of the disasters he had to overcome were of his own making.

Chapter Twelve

My Childhood Before the War

About a foot of fresh powdery snow had fallen during the night covering the little village of Hirschsprung, the valley of the jumping deer, in the Erzgebirge, the Ore Mountains, of Saxony. There was no wind, and the snow lay white and fluffy on the branches of the fir trees making them look like grotesque but friendly figures. Most of the 103 inhabitants were still asleep when the midwife from the next town took out her toboggan during the very early hours of the morning and slid down the hills to the Buschhaus, located in the upper part of the village. A baby was on its way to Gertrud Börner, the wife of the Innkeeper Martin. The little boy arrived on a Sunday at 8 a.m. and, with the help of a few slaps on the bottom, announced to the village with a loud cry that number 104 had checked in. It was November 18, 1929.

Four weeks later at the christening, when the whole family and godparents were assembled in their finery and flowers beautifully decorated the living room, the minister held his sermon. When the moment came to sprinkle water on my forehead, the minister reached into the gold-plated bowl on the table and discovered it was dry. He whispered, "Water, water" to the person next to him, who quietly faded away to get the precious liquid. While waiting, the minister continued the sermon. Seldom did an infant have so many best wishes, until finally the water arrived and the blessings could continue. As the water sprinkled down my forehead and nose, I blew hard and dowsed the bystanders who could do nothing but laugh out loud. I was named Eberhart Martin.

My Earliest Memories—1933

My first memory is having a bath. I loved it, and it happened every Saturday. A wooden washtub was brought up from the *Waschhaus*, a room in the cellar where the washing was done, and brought into the living room. There were no bathrooms with tubs and showers. Then water was heated on the stove in big pots and, when ready, with a lot of huffing and puffing, the water was poured into the wooden tub. When the water was tested for the right temperature, I squealed with delight as I was placed in the waves. I made more waves, splashing everywhere, causing much mopping up later on.

My special fun was sliding back and forth, making big waves that went over the ends. However, the tub was made of wood and splinters quickly pierced my tender bottom. Loud screams brought the family, wondering what the matter was. Only later, when being dried off while still screaming, my father found the splinters sticking out of my behind, whereupon he turned me on my stomach and extracted the intruders. No

Martin's parents Gertrud Schenk and Martin Carl Börner, both born 1890. On their wedding day, December 20, 1920.

more sliding in the tub, until one day I discovered I could slide one way and make waves without getting splinters, and then carefully lift myself off the tub's floor and move back for the next slide. The splashing continued for four more years until a tiled bathroom with tub and shower was installed for the whole house that slept 28 people.

Daily Life

September was blueberry time. The forests were full of bushes with delicious blueberries and people came up from Dresden with pails and jugs to collect the berries. That was the time of my first advertising venture. My mother baked sheets of delicious blueberry cake. When I heard tourists coming down the street, I greeted them and told them how delicious the blueberry cake was, and asked them to come in for a cup of coffee. Many did, and they talked about the little fellow on the street who had sent them into the inn. My mother was proud. But I was after the "fringe" benefits: the crusty borders of the cake were cut off and

Martin and his sister Elfriede in 1931.

not sold, and I always got my share. They were delicious and rich, as the butter from the baking sheet collected in the corners.

That winter my sister Elfriede and my cousin Kate, both five years older, taught me how to ski. They put me on hand-me-down skis that were too long and that had leather bindings that allowed my heel to slip from side to side. Control was limited, but they were the greatest thing for me. With my sister on one hand and my cousin on the other—I was not allowed poles as they were too dangerous—I went up and down the hills with sheer delight. Skiing was a family tradition: my father was on the team that won European cross-country championships in the early 1920s. It was also a necessity, as the village was snowed in for months and the only way to buy groceries was to ski to Altenberg, a mining town of some 2000 souls about three kilometers away.

My grandfather died in 1935. He was a tall man with a bush of white hair and a big smile that was even bigger because he had no teeth left; a horse had kicked them out. His hands were rough like sandpaper, but I loved his touch because it was so reassuring. The year he died, my sister and I went mushroom picking with him.

The village of Hirschsprung lies in a valley close to the top ridge of the Ore Mountains, surrounded by deep forests of spruce and beech where mushrooms grow from July to September. There were many small ones, but some had heads as big as dinner plates. With my grandfather in the middle, me on one side some 10 meters away and my sister on the other, we went into the woods. The best mushroom picking spots were under the branches of young spruce trees. We were looking for *Steinpilze, Braunhaeuptchen, Pfifferlinge,* and *Birkenpilze* mushrooms. Moving through the thick branches, we used our family whistle—da dee da—to orient ourselves. When the other person answered, we could judge how close or far away we were. This whistle had been a family tradition for as long as my grandfather could remember. When we came home, we proudly displayed the mushrooms we had found. My mother cleaned and sliced them and fried some with butter; the aroma still makes my mouth water. Most of them were spread on thick paper and dried for later use. Some mushrooms had maggots, and my sister and I often made bets about which maggot would crawl faster to the edge of the paper and fall off.

With the economy in Germany finally improving, there were more tourists and my parents were very busy, particularly in the summer season, May to September, and in the winter season, December to March. I mostly remember the quiet month of November when we were a family with no guests to interfere. I spent quiet afternoons and evenings tinkering with wood carving or sawing small animals out of sheets of plywood. We painted them, and they miraculously appeared on the Christmas tree on Christmas Eve. My mother was a loving and caring person who spoiled me whenever she had time in the off-seasons. In the main seasons there was no time: she and my father worked from 6 a.m. to 10 p.m. and often later. This was the life of a country inn.

School Days—1936

The first day of school was a great event. To celebrate it and to make me feel better leaving home, or maybe to sweeten the fact that I had to walk three kilometers there and back, I was given a very large *Zuckertuete*, a huge cone filled with candy. The candy was only on top and the rest was stuffed paper—it would have been too heavy otherwise. From then on and for the next eight years, rain or shine, in the most beautiful winter landscapes or in whiteout blizzards, I walked to Altenberg to attend school.

I had a framed slate on which I tried my first letters. The writing was *Siterlin* style, which was the old German way. Three years later we changed the letters to the present Latin style. On this slate I did my first calculations: 1+1=2. (Not like I teach my grandchildren now: 1+1=3. Why? Because you have to make a profit.) My neighbour Helga and my friend Guenther and I walked together to school every day. We normally waited for each other, but if one was late, the other two went ahead and the last one had to run to catch up. I well remember the pencils and slate board and metal sandwich box rattling in the brown leather backpack as I ran, because I was often late. In school, however, we were always the first to arrive, even in the wildest snow storms. The kids living nearby were often late and

Martins first day at school, 1936.

had not fully woken up. We three earned the reputation of being bright and alert. How could you not be after walking three kilometers?

In the afternoons we had to attend a youth group called *Pimpfe*, the youngest group of the Hitler Youth. We wore black shorts, a white shirt, and a brown scarf with a leather knot. We were proud of the uniform; it looked good. We did games and sports, and learned how to march and sing the songs of our country. We accepted the words that did not mean anything to us: *And today Germany belongs to us, and tomorrow the whole world.* Looking back, I realize this youth group was the beginning of a very clever propaganda campaign using nationalism and pride in our homeland to brainwash and mold us into machines. These "machines" later attacked Russian tanks with handheld explosives—run to the tank, stick the charge with magnetic feet onto the wall of the tank, pull the cord, run back to your hole—much like the suicide bombers of the Middle East. Few made it. This was the beginning of my nationalist training. There was more to come.

Pre-War Tensions—1938

The economy further improved. Tour buses came with guests and our dining area was too small, so my father decided to build a verandah connecting to the dining area. It seated about 60 guests. It was the first time that he had the confidence to borrow on a mortgage and invest in the property, the first time since my grandfather built the Buschhaus in 1912 that there was optimism for investment.

The construction was a major event for me. I participated wherever I could, so I thought, but was mostly in the workers' way. The excavation revealed large stones from the foundation, and after a rain we found they contained big veins of amethyst. I wanted to take them out, but my father said, "One day you will own this place and as long as you know where they are, leave them there for now." The excavation also revealed strata lines of different colours like in a riverbed, since that's what it was. When the rains started in the fall, the new foundation wall spewed out water jets over one meter long: the wall was built in an underground stream. Much to my delight, when the underground garage flooded because the drain could not handle the inflow, I commandeered a wooden laundry tub—the one with the splinters—and played canoe using a board for a paddle.

At this time, ethnic tensions increased between the German settlers and the Czechs along the border inside the Czech Republic. Two hundred and fifty years before, the Austrian-Hungarian Empire had defeated the Czechs in a battle, annexed their country, and called it Boehmen, (Bohemia). The King of Boehmen called in German settlers in about 1780 to develop the mostly uninhabited mountain forests along the borders with Germany and

The "Buschhaus" country inn in Hirschsprung, Altenberg, where Martin was born. Built by grandfather Carl in 1912, expanded by Martin's father in 1938.

Ober-Hirschsprung

im Ost-Erzgebirge

English
Girl,

German
Boy

Austria. These people were called the *Sudetendeutschen*. There was always a strong influence of German speaking people in the Czech Republic. Charles University, the oldest German university, was founded in Prague in the 13th century.

In 1938, tensions between the Czechs and the *Sudetendeutschen* developed. I do not know if they occurred naturally or if Hitler provoked them. However, one day my father said there were buses with German refugees coming through on the main road near us between Prague and Dresden. I hopped on the rear seat of his motorbike and we found a bus with refugees going slowly up a hill. My father pulled up by the side of the bus and told me to stand on the bike and look into the bus window. A few seconds later, another bus was coming toward us and a passenger car was squeezing through between the two buses. I crouched down, my father put the brakes on the bike and, as soon as I was clear of the bus with the refugees, I jumped off the bike and landed in the ditch. My father pulled over and shook his head. I had done the right thing, but it was so fast and smooth he could hardly believe it. Later he said, I do not have to worry about Eberhart, he can look after himself. I felt proud.

A few weeks later, German army columns rolled over this road, and in one day occupied the *Sudetenland* to protect the German people there. The rest of the Czech Republic became a Protectorate. Horror stories of the treatment the Sudetendeutschen were used as justification for moving in, and we believed them. Years later, my father said, "If the Western Powers had had the resolve to stop Hitler, it would still have been possible in 1938. But British Prime Minister Neville Chamberlain met Hitler in Munich and naively believed him." Upon his return to London, Chamberlain proclaimed "Peace in our time!"

The Invasion of Poland—1939

The clouds darkened in the summer as reports came of the bad treatment the German-speaking people were receiving in Poland. In September, German troops rolled over the borders and in a few days Poland was defeated. The German government and the Russian government under Stalin divided Poland into two parts, each government occupying the closest part. Subsequently, the Russians deported millions of Poles to labour camps in Siberia where over a million perished.

The Germans and Russians then made a non-aggression agreement to secure the new border. A few days after the invasion of Poland, England and France, who had treaties with Poland, declared war on Germany. World War II had started.

Chapter Thirteen

Life During the War

After four years of public school, my parents felt I should transfer to the Gymnasium, a good boarding school in Altenberg. It was a big change for me. Some of the boarding students were one or two years older and therefore much stronger than me, and they excelled in sports. I was often laughed at because I could not keep up. I excelled only when the winter came and skiing began, because I was born on skis and they came from the lowlands and had no experience with skiing. I was popular in the winter and had a good time. However, as the snow melted in the spring, so melted my popularity; contact sports took over and I was again just a little guy. There were bullies in the class and the little guys suffered a lot from them. Fifty years later, at a class reunion in Altenberg, I met some of these bullies again. All of them were miserable people who had led drab lives, no comparison to my life, which has been very interesting and successful, with much world travel, different languages, and many varied experiences. It just goes to show that it is not how you start the race, IT IS HOW YOU FINISH.

The year 1940 was the year of victories. German armies ran over the Benelux countries, avoiding the heavily fortified Maginot Line at the French-German border, and rolled into France. Later that year, Norway was taken. There seemed to be no way to stop Hitler—he was like a God. The propaganda machine was in full swing, and we youngsters believed what we were told. We had no way of comparing our life with life in other countries. The people who knew were silent because they wanted to be, or more likely because they could not talk because it was too dangerous. Many Germans were hauled off to concentration camps on suspicion of being subversive, never to be seen again.

In 1941, the war was in full swing. Victories occurred on all fronts and most of Europe was occupied by the German army. German intelligence was also aware of what was happening in Russia, where western Allies were massively sending arms and supplies to the arctic ports. A Russian attack on Germany was imminent. When we heard on the radio that Germany had invaded Russia, my father said, "This is impossible to win, this is the beginning of the end." I well remember his sad face.

My cousin Wilfrid, who was then 19 years old and drafted into one of the Panzer Divisions, told me 60 years later, "The first day, we pushed forward from the eastern border of Poland all the way to Kiev, in the heart of the Ukraine. We were refueled by planes dropping barrels of diesel on the side of the road. The Russians were so surprised they fled their tanks and took off into the woods. There were ROWS AND ROWS AND ROWS of tanks standing on the side of the road all pointing west, ready to move into Europe. It was a massive army. Once it would have started rolling, there would have been nothing to stop it. The Soviets would have overrun central Europe all the way to the French coast."

The surprise German attack stopped this Russian push into Europe, only to end four years later after millions and millions of casualties on both sides. Instead, the Russians advanced to the centre of Europe, not to the coast of France. Germany's push into Russia was so swift that supplies could often not follow. The winter of 1941–42 was terribly hard, and the German army was unprepared. I remember we had to collect warm socks and winter clothing to be sent quickly to the front. Like Napoleon 140 years earlier, both armies came to a standstill because of the severity of the Russian winter.

In 1941, German U-boats were at their peak, sinking freighters shipping food and supplies from the USA to an isolated Britain. From Norway to Spain, the coastline was in German hands. Every day we heard *Sondermeldung*, special broadcasts on the radio with fanfares and rousing music—"Today our brave U-boats have sunk 400,000 tons of freighters"—and then more music. Little did I know that my future children's British grandfather was one of the many British Merchant Navy sailors who were torpedoed and drowned in the ice cold waters of the north Atlantic.

The War Continues—1943

The German army was deep into Russia, stopped before St. Petersburg in the north and Moscow in the middle. Stalingrad in the south was taken as it was on the way to Baku on the Black Sea where the oil wells were pumping much-needed fuel. The German advance was stopped east of Stalingrad and the Russians, in a bloody counter-offensive, encircled Stalingrad and the 6th German Army which consisted mostly of soldiers from Saxony. Through the horrible winter of 1943, they were slaughtered. The few Germans who did surrender became prisoners of war, and most died in the Russian camps. The soldiers drafted from our little village were all there. None of them returned.

Yet the propaganda machine was in full swing. We young boys were enthusiastic and ready to die for our fatherland. We had no contact with other countries, no information of what existed in the world beyond our borders. We simply believed what we were told 24 hours a day: the Americans and the English were horrible people, some had horns like the devil, they ate children, they were monsters, etc.

Then I had my first doubts. The German *Luftwaffe* had lost control of the skies and the first allied air raids penetrated deep into Germany. It was a cloudy but bright day when I saw an allied bomber plane appearing out of the clouds. It had a trail of smoke and was losing altitude. Soon several parachutes popped open, and then the plane crashed into the forest about three kilometers away. There was a plume of smoke. I quickly jumped on my bike and headed for the crash site.

I was one of the first to arrive, and I carefully approached the scene. The plane had broken apart, the machine guns were grotesquely pointing towards the sky, ammunition was strewn around, and a fire was smoldering. I saw a man in a blue uniform sitting against a tree with his head dropped to his chest as if he were sleeping. He was part of the crew who did not parachute and had crashed with the plane, been badly hurt, and crawled away from the crash to lean against the tree. I carefully approached him, but he did not move. He was dead. But I remember clearly how I got on my knees and looked into his face from below. What I saw was a good-looking young man with blond hair and blue eyes, a nice face. I thought—*but he looks like us! He doesn't look like a monster.* My first doubts came at that moment. Was all we were told really true? Then the police came and told me to go away. That evening I told my father what I had seen and felt. He replied, "You must not believe everything you hear!" Years later I realized that he could not say more. If he had, and I

The last picture of the family together in Hirschsprung, 1944.

had repeated it to others, he could have been picked up by the police for spreading anti-German propaganda, which was treason. Such people were put in camps, and many were never seen again.

There was much work to do in the *Buschhaus*, our country inn, and we were short of staff. I helped by bringing groceries from Altenberg on my way home from school. I stuffed my schoolbag and a rucksack with the needed items, then rode home quickly on my bicycle. After my homework, I often had to help at the bar and was quite proficient at drafting beer and taking the orders from the waitresses. I also had full control of the cash. Some guests once asked my father how he could entrust such a little boy with so much money. He told them, "No problem. If he needs something he asks me and gets it out of the cash register. I fully trust him!" And so it always was in our family: full trust.

Of course, when a boy is 13 years of age, he feels grown up. I had been a boy soprano in our school choir, but now my voice was all over the octaves. I decided to try smoking. Cigarettes were easily available, and I sold them daily to customers. I locked myself in a toilet and lit up; puffing away, I felt pretty grown up. However, I soon felt sick, my head pounded, and I felt like throwing up. As I snuck out of the toilet, a great cloud of smoke belched out of the door with me. As luck would have it, my father passed by at that moment. He saw the smoke and cornered me. "So," he said, "I see you have been smoking. Well you can smoke ALL you like, but don't you come to me if you are sick!" I felt so sick I could have died. I never smoked a cigarette again in my life.

The Bellevue Hotel, Dresden—1944

The *Buschhaus* was requisitioned by the government as an army hospital; there were simply not enough beds in regular hospitals for all the wounded coming back from the front. My parents, my sister, and I had to move to the top floor and work downstairs for the hospital. I often mixed with the soldiers and talked about the heroic things they had done. I was still convinced our cause was the right one, but doubts began to creep into my indoctrinated mind. How could things be so great if the armies had to retreat and leave behind so many dead comrades? How could so many soldiers be wounded? How could enemy planes fly over us in daylight? What had happened to the U-boats? There were now very few radio announcements about ships being sunk. We did not know it at the time, but the Allies had developed a radar system that could detect U-boats under the sea; now less than 50% returned to base after each mission.

I finished school at Easter. My parents said it was time to learn a trade, just as their fathers and grandfathers had done. "With a trade you can always work and live," they said. To continue school was not really an option. I had no experience to say differently, and I followed their wishes. As they and their parents had all been in the hotel business and someone had to take over the *Buschhaus*, my parents decided to send me to Dresden to the best hotel, the Bellevue, to start my apprenticeship as *Hotelkaufmann*, all-round training for hotel management. My things were packed, my black pants and white jackets bought, the socks and underwear counted by my mother. Then my father brought me to the big city and the hotel.

For the first six months I worked in the restaurant. The headwaiter, a kind, roly-poly man, gave me my first task: washing glasses. I remember so well standing at the sink washing trays full of glasses. I was so alone in the big city and the new world was so different from my little mountain village that I cried, big tears rolling down my cheeks. After awhile the headwaiter returned and kindly said, "*Na ja, so schlimm ist's ja nicht*": Don't be sad, it's not so bad, you will do fine here. He put his hand on my shoulder and gave it a gentle squeeze. That helped—I had found a friend, someone who cared. I then brought the glasses to the restaurant and lined them up on the shelves.

It was such a beautiful place, and I had never seen such splendor. When guests came in, I moved into the corner in shy respect, not wanting to do anything wrong with such fine people. I had been with guests all my life and washed glasses before, but not in such posh surroundings. A week later, I had fully adjusted to my new surroundings. I learned how to set tables and prepare the stations in the restaurant, what to serve when, and I also learned the menus. I loved to hear the guests' conversations: funny and sad stories, but always interesting. As we were not supposed to listen, we could not react to a joke.

One day a week I had to go to trade school where we learned accounting, shorthand, etc. I lived in the hotel under the roof in the staff quarters, three apprentices to one room. My space consisted of a bed and a small locker. Every two weeks I had a day off, and I loved taking the streetcar to the station and then the train for 90 minutes up to the mountains to Altenberg. A 45-minute walk along the familiar road brought me to my Buschhaus, where I was always greeted with hugs and happiness by my mother, father, and sister. I loved to run into the forest, the pine smell of the trees so rich and the air so pure. I jumped over the little hills and rolled in the lush green grass, taking in the smells of pure nature. It was what I had grown up with. This was my world, not the city.

When I was home, I spoke with the wounded soldiers that filled the *Buschhaus* and they told me about the heroic things they did at the fronts. But between their stories were often things they did not want to talk about: lost comrades, whole divisions encircled and decimated. The retreats from the Russian front and in France where the Allies had landed in Normandy were in full swing, called "frontline corrections." I was a bit older now, and with maturity came the thoughts that all was not well and all we were asked to do was not right.

Yet the propaganda continued. Goebbels, the propaganda minister, spoke on the radio, whipping the audience into a state of ecstasy by telling them all the bad things the enemies had done to Germans and the sure victory of the Germanic race. He yelled the famous words, "*Wollt ihr den totalen Krieg*": Do you want total war? And the audience cheered loudly. I remember it clearly. And so it was that we were all in it: men, women, and children. Goebbels once came with his family to the Dresden hotel, when I worked there, and had lunch in the dining room. I was not allowed too close, but I saw his wife and children, and they looked nice to me.

In the fall of 1944, my restaurant time was up and I was transferred to the kitchen. I had to wear checkered pants, a white jacket, and a huge cook's balloon hat. The chef was a big Alsatian man with a mean temper. The first thing he did was turn my balloon hat down to reduce its size: the biggest hat was worn by the chef, not the apprentice! I learned how to peel potatoes and cut vegetables. If the sizes were not correct, the chef screamed at me and more often than not I got a hard slap on my neck so my hat fell off. The chef had only four fingers on one hand, and I could still count them on my skin hours later. In one of his tantrums, he picked up a big casserole and threw it along the floor like a big bowling ball along the side of the long stove where five cooks were working. As the casserole crashed along, each man jumped up in turn. It was funny to see these hopping cooks, but if you were caught laughing you were in real trouble. The sous-chef, or second in command, was Manfred Rytz, a kind man from Switzerland. I became very good friends with him and his family five years later in Zurich.

Duty in the pastry shop included using a three-foot wooden spatula to scrape ice cream off the walls of a copper pot. The pot was half immersed in a salt brine with a below freezing temperature, and it had an axle that was connected to an electric motor on top to rotate the pot. It took about 20 minutes to freeze five litres of ice cream. There was a screw to connect the axle of the pot to the axle of the motor to allow the pot to be removed and cleaned. One day, as I scraped the ice cream off the walls of the pot, this screw got caught in the upturned sleeve of my white

Martin

jacket and twisted it next to my biceps. It hurt like hell, and I still have the scar today. I jammed both feet against the wall of the counter and pushed with full force, ripping the sleeve off the jacket and splitting the seam of the jacket. I landed on my feet in the middle of the room, breathing a sigh of relief. Then I felt a tug on my jacket—the bottom seam was still connected to the turning axle and I was slowly being pulled back to the motor. One final rip took care of this. I walked into the kitchen with my torn jacket

Martin at age 14, a hotel management apprentice, rolling dumplings at the Bellevue Hotel, Dresden. October 1944.

and a bleeding arm. The chef just laughed and said, "You won't do this again, will you?" I got the next two hours off to calm down.

It was now late fall, food was rationed, and we heard that Hamburg, Cologne, and other cities had been bombed. Several nights the sirens sounded, warning of approaching enemy aircraft, but nothing serious happened. Dresden, called the Florence of the North, was a beautiful city full of art and history. It had been spared from bombs so far, and the population honestly felt it was exempt from being attacked because of its beauty and history. Many refugees arrived from the East and were billeted in the city or sent further west.

Food was getting scarce and delicacies were not available for ordinary people. By then I had the confidence of the chef and he often sent me to the cellar with the key to his cooling room to fetch treats for special guests. He thought I was innocent and that his treasures were safe. A box of smoked eels—a rare delicacy— was in the cooling room, becoming moldy over time. When I had to fetch one, the mould was wiped off and it was sold as fresh. I could not bear to see beautiful eels rotting away, so I hatched a plan. I put a strong string around my waist with two loops above my pant legs. The next day when I was sent into the cool room to fetch an eel, I took two good-sized eels and stuck them into the loops, tying them firmly at the neck so they dangled inside my pant legs. My apron covered the theft well.

When the shift was over, I left the hotel with two eels sloshing inside my pants to avoid showing them in my bag to the guard at the door. On the train home, I removed the eels and put them into my bag.

My parents were delighted with the rare gift, but of course I did not tell them where I got it. I justified my action by telling myself that I was getting back at the chef who had hit me once too often. Years later I found out that he was extremely unhappy at home so he took it out on the apprentices.

Christmas came and luckily, as the youngest apprentice, I got the day off. When I arrived home on the evening of the 23rd, it was a fairyland of snow— deep powder and not too cold. Our rooms upstairs were warm and decorated with angels, the *Rauchermanner* (small hollow wooden figures) blowing incense into the air, the Christmas tree laden with home-made ornaments. My sister Elfriede, then 20 years old, my parents in their mid-fifties, and I were all together. They called me *Herzenjunge tralala*, meaning boy of my heart-tralala, because when I was little my mother always hugged and kissed me and called me that. We had a great Christmas Eve with carol singing and pres-ents, even if they were small, full of love and security as only you can feel in a warm family. It was the last Christmas we ever had together as a family.

New Year's Eve in the Bellevue Hotel was a busy night. The celebration was in full swing and we apprentices thought we had a reason to celebrate too. We took several bottles of red wine and made a punch with cherries. As the wine was a little dry, we sweet-ened it with plenty of sugar. We drank with youthful exuberance until 2 a.m. When my shift started at 9 a.m., I could barely get up: my head was spinning, I threw up, I was ready to die, but the shift had to go on. When the chef arrived at 10 a.m., he took one look at my white face and laughed out loud: "So you think you are such a big man, hey; everybody, look at the big man, he can't even drink a glass of wine. Look how pale he is, his legs are crumbling!'" And so it went on for hours as I stumbled from one sink to the other to throw up. I never felt so humiliated and swore then that I would never, never get that drunk again and lose control.

The Bombing of Dresden—1945

In the middle of January my father came to Dresden to visit me. In my afternoon hours off, between the lunch and dinner shift, we walked around the most beautiful part of Dresden. The Bellevue Hotel stood between the famous *Semper* Opera building and the Elbe River. Nearby was the *Zwinger*, an art gallery of beautiful baroque design. Fountains and reflecting pools were in the centre of a very large court. It is said that the Hermitage in St. Petersburg, the Louvre in Paris, and the Dresden Zwinger are the three leading art galleries in the world.

Next to the *Zwinger* was the *Schloss*, the castle of the Saxon kings, and next to it the *Hofkirche*, a Catholic church built by August the Strong who convert-ed to Catholicism in the late 18th century. Legend has it that he had 365 children; thereafter, many Saxons, including myself, claim that they most likely have royal blood in their veins. On the parapet of the roof of the church, thirty larger than life statues of saints were built to look down onto the mortals. Opposite the church was the *Augustusbruecke*, the bridge leading over the Elbe River to *Neustadt*, the newer part of Dresden. Walking across the bridge, I pointed out an iron door to my father, about one metre square on the side of the stone wall of the riverbank next to the hotel. I told him this door was one of the exits from the wine cellar that served as an air raid shelter for the hotel guests and staff.

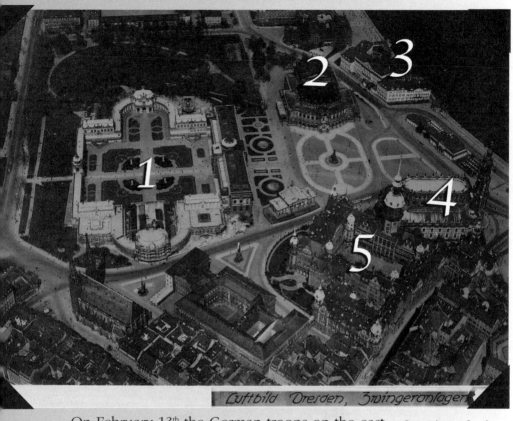

Luftbild Dresden, Zwingeranlagen

On February 13th the German troops on the eastern front had retreated to Breslau. The war was clearly lost. Streams of refugees from the east flowed into Dresden, and every school, hospital, and available house was packed full. They thought that since Dresden was whole and had been spared from bombing so far, it would not be bombed and they were safe.

Pre-war historic Dresden:
(1) Zwinger;
(2) Semper Opera House;
(3) Bellevue Hotel;
(4) Catholic Hof Kirche;
(5) Castle of Saxon Kings.

At 9:45 p.m., the air raid sirens sounded. I was in the kitchen finishing up. We thought it was just another alarm—they happened twice a week. As I belonged to one of the fire fighting units, I put on my brown overalls and steel helmet, strung the round container with the gas mask over my shoulder, and went into the shelter. Shortly after, one of the senior men came down the stairs and said, "It's a big raid, the

Christmas trees are all over the sky!" Christmas trees were clusters of flares on small parachutes. They were

Hof Kirche, Castle and Semper Opera House.

dropped as markers, indicating where the bombers which followed were to unload their cargo. This was not a precision bombing raid on military targets. This was a blanket bombing raid designed to start huge fires and to kill as many people as possible to demoralize the enemy.

And then it started: boom, boom, and boom— not bad we thought. We did not know that a rain of incendiary bombs had hit the city. After 30 minutes it calmed down and the main warden, my roly poly head-waiter, said to me: "Go to the roof and report any damage." As I ran up the stairs, I put on my gas mask. The top floor was full of smoke. A young fellow from Holland was there clutching a column and sliding down, overcome by smoke. I do not know how he got there, but he had no gas mask and was obviously suffocating. I grabbed him, dragged him to the wide carpeted hotel stairs, and rolled him down. I remember he bounced down the stairs onto a landing, where the air was still clear. He got up on wobbly feet and continued down. I never saw him again.

I found the door to the attic, climbed a wooden stair, and looked both ways. There was fire everywhere. Within seconds I stepped down the stairs, only to find the side of the stairs was already on fire. Liquid phos-

Bellevue Hotel on the Elbe River and Semper Opera House.

phorous (like napalm) dropped in canisters had burst on impact, splashing the oozy liquid everywhere and quickly igniting when it mixed with oxygen. Running down to the warden, I reported the whole roof was on fire. He said, run to the police station at the *Schloss Strasse*

1943 British Royal Air Force aerial photos, preparing for 1945 bombing raid. (1) location of Bellevue Hotel.

(GERMANY)

0   500   1000   1500   2000 YARDS

0   1 MILE

(1 : 24,800)   approx.

Issued November 1943

2400 Yds

Luftaufnahme der RAF von Dresden mit eingezeichnetem Zielsektor. Vom heutigen Heinz-Steyer-Stadion ausgehend, umfaßt er das kulturhistorische Zentrum und die Wohnviertel der Altstadt

and report the hotel is on fire. This I did, running with all my speed past the *Hofkirche*, when all of a sudden I fell flat on my stomach. I turned around to see why I had tripped. I had tripped over a head. It was the head of one of the statues on the roof of the Hofkirche which had come loose in the bombing tremors. I continued to the fire station and reported the hotel on fire. The officer said, "Yes, the Bellevue Hotel and the whole city." I returned and reported this back to the warden. There was a sad silence, and then he shouted orders for the rescue of people and for the fire hoses to be in place to start the fight.

We pulled the fire hoses up the staircases. There was a lot of smoke, and I still had my gas mask on. I stood in a doorway facing a whole room of fire; the heat was intense. The hose had good water pressure which I directed into the flames, but it was like a drop onto a hot stone: the flames just roared. Then I heard or sensed some cracking above me. I stepped back and the door frame collapsed, burying my hose. I pulled the hose out from under the hot rubble, climbed on it, and continued dowsing the fire. This was what we had been trained to do: you got an order and you obeyed it with total disregard for your own safety. After 15 minutes, the warden came up and waved at me to come down to the lower levels, probably saving my life.

After ensuring all the people were out of the building, we tried to save some bedding and mattresses which we put on the ground. But it was useless: the sparks were flying everywhere and the wind blew too strongly from the storm. We put mattresses on the ground near the Opera house next door which was also on fire. There was a tremendous roar over the opera house, like a huge blowtorch blowing to the sky. The incendiary bombs had penetrated the roof and fallen

English Girl, German Boy

BOMBERSTROM

8000 mtr
RADIO-FLUGZEUGE

WETT

SICHTPRÜFER

ZIELMARKIERER

MASTERBOMBER

RADARMARKIERER
BELEUCHTER
ZIELMARK.-BOMBEN

DRESDEN

Wie Dresden starb...

Masterbomber Maurice Smith stürzt mit seiner Mosquito aus...

Aber noch etwas stellt der Master-bomber fest. Nach seinen Informatio-nen sollen sich durch Dresden mehrere deutsche Armeen zur Ostfront wäl-zen. Doch kein einziges Flakgeschütz eröffnet das Feuer auf den tief-fliegenden Schnell-Bomber. Kein ein-ziger Scheinwerfer versucht, ihn mit seinem Lichtfinger zu fassen.

Dresden ist ohne jede Verteidi-gung...

In wenigen Minuten laufen nun die komplizierten Vorbereitungen ab mit...

„Hallo, Hauptmarkierer!" ruft Oberst-leutnant Smith. „Können Sie die grünen Leuchtbomben erkennen?"

„Ja, ich sehe deutlich einen grünen Schimmer durch die Wolkendecke", antwortet die Stimme des Haupt-markierers, dessen Mosquito noch in sechstausend Meter Höhe fliegt.

„Dann kommen Sie herunter und markieren Sie den Zielpunkt", be-fiehlt der Masterbomber.

Jetzt rast die Mosquito des Haupt-markierers im Sturzflug auf Dresden...

„Rote Zielma
Wolken noch de

Es ist genau
Lautsprechern u
jetzt eine aufg
tung, Achtung!
lichen Bomber
im Anflug auf
mit Bombenabw
Bevölkerung wi
die Luftschutzr
sich jetzt noch
wird von der Pc

into the seats of the opera, igniting the dry wood. The walls of the building were of thick solid stone and survived, and are still there today. The windows were broken and the fire sucked the air through the windows to supply oxygen to the inferno inside. I saw trees as thick as a thigh bending 90 degrees as their branches were sucked into the window. When I saw one of the mattresses we had put on the ground flying through the air

RADARMARKIERER

Die Perfektion der Ver
Bei ihren Nachtangriffen auf Dre
und taktische Methoden an, die
geklügelt worden waren. Und a
rechts wurde kurz vor dem Eintr
Mosquito aufgenommen. Die „B
Stadion ist taghell erleuchtet. Je
bombe ausgelöst (Pfeil). Sie wi

jedoch stehen alle andere
räume des Hospizes in h
men.

and being sucked into the window, I decided it was time to go into the shelter. We could not do much more.

No sooner did I get to the shelter when the air raid sirens howled again for the second raid. The Christmas trees came again, and then the block-buster bombs. The Allies' plan was to first set the city on fire with incendiary bombs, and then with the second attack use explosives to shatter the remaining windows so the blowing sparks could set the buildings on fire. It succeeded. The Dresden firestorm was in full swing.

There were only about 15 people in our shelter. The others had escaped to the banks of the Elbe River or tried to go to their homes and families. We were huddled on the floor when I heard the inside steel door of our exit slapping because it was not closed. I got up, pushed the door closed, and pushed the big levers into closed position. Shortly after, there was a huge bang, and we bounced two feet from the floor as the shockwave hit. A bomb had exploded close to the door, but the door held. I still wonder today, would our lungs have survived the air pressure if the door had been open? When the rumbling finally stopped, I fell

Execution of the bombing raid. A ring of "Christmas trees" - flares on parachutes -was dropped by marker planes to show the closely following bombers where to unload their cargo anywhere in the circle.

asleep totally exhausted, only to wake up five hours later when I felt a tap on my shoulder. It was my father who said, "Come, it's time to go home."

The night before, my father was in the *Buschhaus* about 35 km south of Dresden in the mountains when he saw the sky turning bright red on the horizon above Dresden. When he heard the rumbling of the explosions, he said to my mother, "I have to go to Dresden to get our boy out." All he had was an old bicycle which he rode to the edge of town, arriving about 8 a.m. The town was a sheet of flames, and he thought, "My God, will I find my boy alive?"

He searched for an open street to get to the hotel at the river, but could not find one because the heat was too intense. He heard a voice calling for help and turned around

One of the surviving statues of saints on the parapet of the church overlooking the destroyed city, asking "why?"

and found a man half covered by rubble. He pulled him out. Seconds later, the façade of a burning house in front of him collapsed, just where he would have been had he not helped the man. He took his scarf, wet it, and put it in front of his nose to keep the smoke out. Finally he found the *Grosse Garten*, a long park leading from the outskirts to the river Elbe. He walked to the river and then along the bank toward the hotel. When

he arrived, he saw the hotel had collapsed.
Remembering where I had pointed out the exit door on
the side of the riverbank leading to our shelter, he found
the door, removed some rubble, opened it to climb in
and found people huddled on the floor. He asked if
anyone had seen Eberhart. The warden was there and
said, "Yes, he is sleeping in there, but let him sleep, he
has done so much; we would not be alive if he had not

been here." My father replied he had come to take me home, and the warden agreed. I waved goodbye as I left—I never saw the warden again.

We walked along the riverbank to the area where my father had come through the town. People were sitting against walls or lying on the ground as if they were sleeping, but all were dead. I remember a

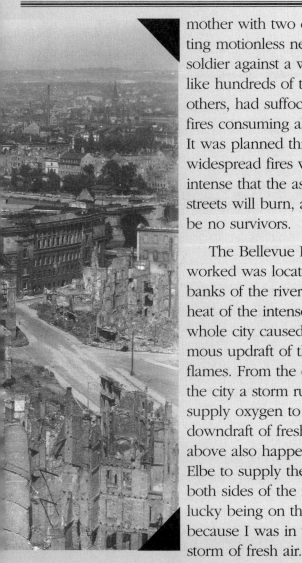

mother with two children sitting motionless next to an old soldier against a wall. They, like hundreds of thousands of others, had suffocated from the fires consuming all the oxygen. It was planned this way: create widespread fires with heat so intense that the asphalt on the streets will burn, and there will be no survivors.

The destroyed historic city. (1) location of the collapsed Bellevue Hotel.

The Bellevue Hotel where I worked was located on the banks of the river Elbe. The heat of the intense fires of the whole city caused an enormous updraft of thundering flames. From the outskirts of the city a storm rushed in to supply oxygen to the fires. A downdraft of fresh air from above also happened over the Elbe to supply the fires on both sides of the river. I was lucky being on the riverbank because I was in the incoming storm of fresh air.

As my father and I walked through the burned out streets we came to a railroad underpass where people had sought shelter. All were dead. We had to step over the bodies. The Russian front had advanced to 80 kilometers from Dresden, and millions of refugees were fleeing the Russians. At the time of the bombings, Dresden was packed with refugees in private homes, public buildings, anywhere where shelter could be found from the February cold. Dresden was not a military target except for the railroad bridges, which ironically remained intact.

The YALTA conference took place from February 7–11, 1945. Did Churchill and Roosevelt sacrifice the pawn of Dresden to appease Stalin? The total destruction of the city two days after the conference cannot be a coincidence! The Allies knew the city was packed with refugees. Stalin had asked for help, and they saw their chance to demoralize the people of Germany by killing as many civilians as possible. I have always believed that refugees are already demoralized...

17 square kilometres of the city, packed with refugees, burned in one day. The most deadly firestorm in history.
The intense fires consumed the oxygen, and there were few survivors.

We came to the railroad station, the *Hauptbahnhof*. Bodies were everywhere. Later we heard that the large shelters near there had been packed with people, and nobody had survived. It was about 1 p.m. as we headed up the hill past the university, and then to the high ground where Napoleon had fought a battle on his retreat from Russia. We looked back over the city: smoldering ruins as far as the eye could see. Thirty minutes later the road was

packed with fleeing survivors from the outskirts pushing
carts and clutching children and a few belongings, then
we heard the sirens again. It was the start of the third
wave of bombers, which lasted about half an hour. In
search for shelter, my father and I crawled into a
drainage culvert under the road where we felt the

shockwaves of the explosions which pushed us from side to side. "God, isn't it enough?!" When the noise calmed down, we continued our trek home, arriving after dark. My mother was so happy she hugged me again and again and said she had been praying all day for our safe return.

At the ceremony commemorating the 60th anniversary of the fire bombing of Dresden in June

2005, I learned that the first and second raids consisted of 1,400 RAF (Royal Air Force) bombers, and that the third raid consisted of 2,250 American bombers. Imagine the explosive power of the bombs of one plane, then imagine ten, a hundred, a thousand planes, and finally 3,650 planes dropping bombs on mostly refugees within the space of fifteen hours—only then will you comprehend the enormity of this mass murder.

Well-known journalist Doug Saunders wrote the following article in Canada's national newspaper, The *Globe and Mail*, to commemorate the 60th anniversary of the bombing of Dresden. He has given permission for us to reprint it here.

Altmarkt, Dresden, February–April, 1945. The bodies were piled on large grills and burned. The sheer volume made identification impossible. We smelled the sweet smell of burning human flesh for months in the mountains 35 km away. The estimated number of dead is well over 100,000.

A family in a shelter, the mother bending over her baby in the carriage.
All suffocated - there was no oxygen to breathe.

Lessons of Dresden are much misremembered

DOUG SAUNDERS
12 February 2005
The Globe and Mail

Even as it was taking place, 60 years ago this weekend, it was quite obvious to everyone that what was occurring in Dresden was the worst kind of mistake.

A few days after the firebombing began on the night of Feb. 13, 1945, a Toronto resident named A.G.F. Sutton wrote a letter to The Globe and Mail: "It is very disconcerting to learn from the press that the Allies have decided to engage in 'terror bombing' of Germany, in order to hasten the end of the war.

"However bitter we may feel toward Germany and her people, two wrongs do not make a right. . . . We believe we are fighting for Christian principles. Let us, therefore, conduct ourselves accordingly."

People in the civilian world had not been told at that point that as many as 100,000 people, mostly cowering women and children, were being very deliberately burned to death in bomb-fed storms of flame that eliminated the entire German city. They had not been told that Dresden was targeted precisely because it had no major military targets, and therefore had not been bombed before, and therefore was packed with civilian refugees. They did not know that the chief goal of the operation was to create so much horror that civilians would be demoralized.

But people were able to figure those things out. The words "mass murder" were being thrown about in the days immediately after the terror-bombing campaign, by reasonable people in Canada and Britain and the United States.

People knew about the vicissitudes of war, having endured it, and lost family members to it, for six years. Citizens were well aware that even the noblest military actions would end up killing some innocent people. You didn't hear people arguing that military actions were wrong because a few innocent bystanders might be killed, or the odd wedding party struck by a stray bomb.

But that also allowed them to recognize that what was happening in Dresden was different. This was the deliberate, mass killing of civilians. Some soldiers might also die, but that would be a lucky accident.

People in Canada gleaned the truth when they saw this paper's coverage in the days after the attack. "Ten enemy cities shuddered to the roar of Allied bombs," a front-page story read.

"The weight of the attacks was

against Dresden, a refugee-jammed industrial and communications centre of
Saxony. . . .

"Dresden was hit three times within
15 hours — twice by the RAF in a 1,400-
plane operation Tuesday night that started the assault rolling, and again by
Britain-based bombers of the (American)
8th Air Force, which staged a 2,250-plane
daylight follow-up."

A few days later, under the banner
front-page headline, Plan 'Terror-Bombing'
of Germany, the paper offered this lead:
"The Allied air chiefs have made the
long-awaited decision to adopt deliberate
terror bombing of the great German population centres as a ruthless expedient to
hasten Hitler's doom. . . . Their avowed
purpose will be creating more confusion
in the German traffic tangle and sapping
German morale. . . .

"The decision may revive protests
from some Allied quarters against 'unciv-
ilized warfare,' but they are likely to
be balanced by satisfaction in those sections of Europe where the German Air
Force and the Nazi V-weapons have been
responsible for the indiscriminate slaugh-
ter of civilians by tens of thousands."

There, while the scorched corpses
were still being pitchforked onto train
cars in Dresden, was the crux of all the
arguments over the morality of warfare
that have taken place over the interven-

ing six decades.

We like to think that deep concern over civilian casualties in wars is an affectation of today's sensitized world. It is often said by conservative historians that the use of Dresden as an example of inappropriate targeting of civilians was something that emerged during Vietnam or Iraq, an ass-backward rereading of history to justify today's arguments and values.

In fact, the opposite is true. Today's debates about civilian deaths in Najaf and Kosovo and Kabul were played out in full, at the very moment that Dresden was occurring. The difference was not that other moral standards existed then. Ever since Hugo Grotius began writing about the subject in the early 1600s, it has been clear that civilians should not be targets in war. And they weren't, with few exceptions, until the 20th century.

The "area bombing" campaign, which included atrocious civilian killings in Frankfurt, Berlin, Tokyo and (using different technology) Hiroshima and Nagasaki, has provided two generations of philosophers and ethicists with fundamental questions: To what extent can you commit evil acts, as evil as those committed by your enemy, if they might justify a greater good? And how many wrongs can you commit and still claim that your cause is right?

Dresden and the other horrors of 1945 were so extreme, so deeply immoral, that they have polluted two generations of thought about war. They have created two false assumptions.

The first is that there cannot be a just war, one fought with moral limits: We should abandon the laws of war, and use our enemy's worst techniques. This theory led to My Lai and Abu Ghraib.

The opposing conclusion is that even one civilian death is unacceptable and all war is wrong. This thought has led people to condemn acts of considerable good like the Afghanistan and Kosovo campaigns, and to tolerate great atrocities in Rwanda and Iraq, on the grounds that any ill effects of taking action are unacceptable.

But the lesson of Dresden is that a war can be completely right while any number of its decisions can be murderous, criminal, utterly immoral, atrocious.

The knowledge of these atrocities does not mean we have to shut ourselves off from the world. There is a big difference between civilians being killed during a campaign that is otherwise well intended, and the deliberate targeting of civilians to create terror.

Roy Akehurst, a wireless operator on that night 60 years ago, knew immediately

English
Girl,

German
Boy

that this moral boundary had been crossed. "I found myself making comments to the crew — 'Oh God, those poor people,' " he told one historian, "It was completely uncalled for. You can't justify it."

He was right then, and we are right now: Such things are completely uncalled for.

dsaunders@globeandmail.ca

Document GLOB000020050212e12c00022

The loss of one life is tragic. So is the loss of 10, 100, or 1000 lives. To put it in perspective, in Hiroshima about 66,000 lives were lost; in Nagasaki, about 39,000. In Dresden, it can only be estimated that between 200,000 and 300,000 people died in 15 hours, making it the largest man made loss of civilian life in one day. In the history of man there are many examples of man's inhumanity to man: Dresden is one of its most infamous.

To clean up the bodies, sections of streetcar tracks were welded into the shape of a large grill; the bodies piled on it, and set on fire. Burning human flesh smells sweet, and for months we smelled the burning 35 kilometers away in the mountains. When Churchill heard of the devastating effect of the firestorm and the enormous civilian casualties, he forbade any publicity about it. It was only many years after the war that the world heard about Dresden, and then only in bits and pieces. The publicity of The Holocaust overshadowed it.

The rule of law should govern man. The Nazi leadership was put on trial at Nuremberg. What about the planners of these firestorm air raids designed to kill as many civilians as possible to demoralize the enemy? Are they murderers? Why was bomber Arthur Harris, who was part of the planning group of these firestorm air raids, honored some 50 years later with a "hero's" monument in London? Is there a law for the victorious and another for the vanquished? How can mankind evolve in a civilized way without one law for all? These questions are still unanswered as man's inhumanity to man continues today.

Historians have stated that there was an understanding between nations in Europe not to target civilians during conflicts. After the German occupation of France, the Benelux countries and Norway in 1940, there was a quiet period. Winston Churchill needed to rally the allies and goaded Adolf Hitler into action by bombing civilian targets in Berlin. Thereupon, Hitler sent a number of diplomats to Churchill to reconfirm the original understanding not to bomb civilians. Churchill ignored it and bombed Berlin several more times.

In response, Hitler ordered the first bombing of London in 1940. In 1941, Hitler's deputy, Rudolf Hess, flew to Scotland and offered to withdraw from France, the Benelux countries and Norway in exchange for peaceful co-existence with Great Britain. It had become evident that the communist Soviet Union in the East was the real enemy of Europe.

Churchill ignored these approaches and continued the bombing of German cities. It was only then that Hitler ordered the V1 and V2 rockets to target Britain. ("V" means Vergeltung" or "tit-for-tat").

There was a brief opportunity to prevent the many civilian casualties on both sides. Churchill did not take it.

Chapter Fourteen

The War Ends—1945

I stayed at home recovering for two weeks. I talked to the wounded soldiers in the *Buschhaus*. Their stories became more dramatic, but they could not say all they wanted. I sensed they knew the war was lost. They hoped their wounds would heal slowly so they would not have to go to the front again. All were afraid of the advancing Russians. They knew what it meant to be occupied by them, and they were trying to get transferred to the West.

Yet the propaganda machine rolled on. The *Fuehrer* had a secret weapon that could change everything: they were working on nuclear bombs and came close, but could not get them finished (thank God). Then I was called to the Hitler youth training camp near Altenberg, where we received full military training at age 15. The propaganda continued and welded us into a fighting force to save our fatherland. Those over 55 were recruited into the militia, called the *Volkssturm*, the people's storm.

One day a high ranking officer came to the camp. We stood at attention in formation while he gave us a fiery speech: "You are the hope of the Fatherland, every single one has to do his duty to the *Fuehrer*." He built us up and then asked us to volunteer to fight on the Russian front to protect our country. All who volunteered were asked to step one step forward. All did except a friend of mine and myself. The officer was raving mad, as he had expected the whole unit to volunteer. My friend and I were put in front facing the others and we were screamed at and berated for being the cowards of the group while the others were the heroes of the Fatherland. We felt terrible.

The next day I met my old biology teacher who was in charge of the militia unit in Altenberg, and I asked him if he needed me to help him. He replied that he needed a messenger with a bike, and ordered me to report to him the next morning. I asked him to notify my unit and request a transfer and he agreed. The next morning I reported to him for duty, however somehow the request for my transfer did not arrive at my unit. That morning, a detachment of four members of my unit arrived at my father's house to find me. I had not reported for duty and was therefore a deserter, particularly since I had not volunteered the day before. They had loaded rifles and orders to shoot me, and they would have shot me on the spot had they been able to find me; this was the level of indoctrination they were under. Yet these were my classmates I had grown up with! It took all of my father's persuasion to convince them I was requisitioned by the militia, serving the Fatherland, and that there must be some mistake. Shortly after, my unit was moved to the front at Breslau where 30% died in the last days of the war.

My sister Elfriede was then 21 years of age. She had black hair and dark eyes, a striking-looking young lady. We had a lot of fun together, although sometimes I teased her too much and she got mad. A year earlier she had met an engineer of the merchant navy from Hamburg. He had been on a ship which was sunk in the fjord of Narvik in Norway. He was rescued from the icy waters, but suffered a broken leg which had healed together without being properly stretched. As a result, he had a short leg and limped. Otherwise he looked dashing.

It was now the end of April 1945. They decided to marry, and my parents scrambled to put a little party together. My father had hidden away a few bottles of wine. The morning of the wedding when he went to bring them up from the cellar, he discovered the lock had been broken and the wine stolen by one of the many wounded soldiers in the house. The wedding went on with beer. It was the last wedding in the old church in Altenberg before it was burned down in the last days of the war.

My father sensed that all was not right between the young couple and told my sister that she could stay home and let him leave for the West alone. But she decided against it. Surely the advancing Russian army was a consideration. They got to Berlin and caught the last train out of Berlin to Hamburg. It was strafed by low flying fighter planes, but got through before Berlin was surrounded by the Russian army. My sister had a difficult life. Her husband was at sea and she raised four children by herself. He never gave her sufficient household money, and she had to work odd jobs, even when the children were small. But the worst was that he was a pedophile who abused even his own girls. Twenty-five years later my sister finally got a divorce, but the unhappiness and the mental pressure of all those years took their toll. She died at age 55 of liver cancer. Her husband then married a bossy woman who took everything he owned, and he died miserably 15 years later.

I did my duty as a messenger for the militia in Altenberg and whizzed around on my bike. The main road from Dresden to Prague goes through Altenberg. In those final weeks of the war, the road was packed with retreating military units and refugees with horse-drawn wagons, pushcarts, baby carriages, anything with wheels. Everyone wanted to get away from the Russians and go to the advancing Americans who were already in Bavaria and in Czechoslovakia near Prague. This retreating mass included General Wlassow and his army of Ukrainians and Russians who had fought on the German side for the liberation of their country from Stalin. They reached the Americans and surrendered to them. Within a month, the Americans turned all of them over to the Russians. They were never heard from again: they were all shot.

Mosquito fighter planes machine gunned and bombed the retreating columns of soldiers and refugees, leaving burned out cars and bodies of soldiers and civilians all along the road. One day I wanted to have a closer look at the column and snuck through some bushes close to the road. Concentrating on the road ahead of me, I stumbled over something; it was a man's leg. Then I saw a pile of excrement covered with two hundred Mark bills which had been used as toilet paper as it was worthless money. The 1000 year old Reich was over after only 12 years.

On May 5, just after I reported for duty in the *Rathaus*, the City Hall, I heard the scream of falling bombs. I was in the middle of the ground floor with 12 people in the room. We dropped to the floor and three bombs hit very close on the sides of the house. The windows blew in, part of the ceiling fell down, everyone yelled "get out, get out." But some inner voice told me to lie down. The others stepped over me to run to the front door and out of the building. Within seconds, another bomb fell on the street in front of the building, killing everyone.

My inner voice then told me to get out now. I got up and ran to the front door where four steps led down to the street. Standing on top of the steps, I saw a mass of twitching bodies. A woman lifted her head, a fountain of blood gushing from her neck. The image is still burnt in my mind. I jumped over her, running away from the building up a hill to the outskirts of the town. Near my uncle's bakery, I fell down. I had stumbled over a hipbone. My hands felt soft, warm flesh. A bomb had fallen there too and had killed many people. Looking up, I saw a dead soldier sitting bent forward with a gun on his belt. I rushed over and cut his belt with my pocket knife as I did not want to turn him over. In anger, I took his gun, leaned against a tree, and emptied the magazine shooting at the planes still circling above. My shots did not even tickle them, but I got rid of some of my frustrations.

When the planes left, I walked home to *Hirschsprung.* I had lost my bike. My parents asked why I was so bloody, and I told them about my jump from the top of the steps of the *Rathaus* over the dying woman; I was covered with her blood. Big billows of smoke could be seen over Altenberg where the bombing had set the town on fire. The church went up in flames. We were stunned. The wounded soldiers in the *Buschhaus* were packed on horse drawn wagons confiscated from the farmers in a last effort to reach the Americans, or *Amis* as we called them, and not fall into Russian hands. My aunt Senda from Dresden, along with her very stately 85-year-old husband who was a former judge, had taken refuge with us. They decided to flee and went walking on the road to Prague. They came back within an hour, as he could not make it up the hill to Altenberg. They said, if we have to die, then it is better here than on the road.

On the afternoon of May 6, soldiers were fleeing everywhere with any transport they could find. A colonel had taken quarters at the *Forsthaus,* the large forest administration offices near us, and he decided to make a stand against the Russians. He collected a ragtag group of fleeing solders to build a line of defense in our village. My father was against it because if there was resistance, the Russian artillery would level every house. That evening he visited the colonel and they talked strategy. The soldiers were camping nearby. The colonel had some schnapps and they toasted to the future of the Fatherland. More schnapps followed, heroic songs were sung, and then more schnapps. My father went to the washroom and very quietly told the solders to disappear, to fade into the dark. They did not have to be told twice. The line of last defense never materialized. In the end, there was just a drunk colonel with his driver and my father. The colonel decided to move on too. The war was over.

My father walked home to the *Buschhaus*, and having had a lot of schnapps himself, he loudly sang the songs of our *Heimat*, folk songs of the *Erzgebirge*. The sound echoed down the valley, then four shots rang out. The next morning we found out that a neighbour, an ardent member of the party, had shot his wife, daughter, granddaughter and himself. He did not want to live without the Third Reich and couldn't bear to fall into Russian hands. Other rumors went around the village that these neighbors had sung first and then shot themselves, but it was my father who had sung the songs. In the morning my father took me to their house, saying I had to see the end of an era. The man was sitting in the middle of the bed with his uniform on, his gun in his hand. He and his family had bullets in their heads. I remember the little three-year-old girl, her blond hair mixed with the crusted blood which had run down her cheek.

English
Girl,

German
Boy

The Russians Arrive

On the morning of May 7, I looked out of the window down the road to the village and saw horses and wagons. The people had all the same brown clothes on, not the usual mixture of colors worn by refugees. I yelled into the house, the Russians are coming! The Russians are coming! Within minutes, the road and parking area in front of our house were filled with wagons and soldiers. They stopped to have a bivouac, a rest. A horse-drawn field kitchen, a big kettle with fire underneath, drew up. The soldiers came into our house and looked at every room. Some sat on the lawn in front of our house. Some spoke German, so my father and I went out and talked to them. They told us they were the advanced fighting group and to put anything valuable and the women away because after them would come the robbers and thieves. They were so right!

A horse-drawn field kitchen pulled up, smoke bellowing from the short chimney. We had not had a warm meal for days. I took a pot out of the kitchen and lined up with the soldiers for food. I was last. I can still remember the round moon face of the cook standing high above me swinging a big ladle. He gave me a broad smile and ladled about a gallon of soup into my pot. I smiled back and thanked him. I went into the house where my parents and I sat on the stairs and, each with a spoon in hand, ate the soup. It tasted good: beans, potatoes, and beef chunks.

Somehow two horses spooked and galloped away, pulling their wagon with the soldiers' equipment on it. About six soldiers got up and ran after the wagon. They followed it over the fields until one of them gained control of the horses. Their orders were to stay with their equipment—amazing discipline. What good is a soldier without a rifle? An hour after they left, other soldiers came in small groups. They yelled biwa, biwa, which is beer. Of course there was none, and they got mad. Weeks later we figured out that the empty beer barrels standing in view had made them stop. After we hid the barrels behind the house we had fewer "visitors."

One of the soldiers saw my accordion case under my bed, pulled it out, and with a big smile sat on my bed and started playing. I just stood there. When he was finished, he took it with him. My uncle, the judge, had a pocket watch with a gold chain across his stomach, which a soldier ripped off; my uncle could not get over it for days. One night we heard banging on the front door and when I went to see who it was and shone my flashlight through the glass, I saw Mongolian-looking Russian soldiers. I had to let them in. First they grabbed my flashlight, and then they went through the house. Every night we took in refugees, and the floor of the restaurant was full of them sleeping among their sparse belongings. The soldiers grabbed two women and dragged them screaming to the little entrance hall where they were raped by the lot. I did not fully know what was happening. I was standing on the other side of the door, hearing it all. I will never forget the thump, thump, thump and the whimpering of the women behind the door. Then we heard a shot in the kitchen. I thought my father was dead. A soldier had fired a shot into the floor to scare everybody. The next day we dug the bullet out of the floor.

These visits continued daily and we were helpless. It's a horrible feeling to be totally at another's mercy. To protect the women from falling into the Russian soldier's hands, we devised a warning system. We hung a steel T-bar on a tree and as soon as someone saw a car coming down the road, this T-bar was banged hard with a steel pipe. It sounded like a church bell. Others below in the valley heard it and banged their T-bar and so the whole village sounded its warning bells. Then the women disappeared into the attics, behind trap doors, or into the woods, since we knew the soldiers did not like to go into the woods.

One day a car with soldiers drove into the village below us. In one house there was a woman about to give birth. The few men left in the village decided to come together at her house to protect the woman just by being there, hoping the soldiers would go away. The soldiers went away, but not before beating up the old men. A few minutes later I saw my father staggering up the hill, his face bleeding. He said that as he was being beaten, he tried to hold the soldier's arms, but when he noticed the soldier going for his gun he let go—it was better to be beaten than to be shot.

Food was very sparse. Horses and cows had been stolen, and there was hardly a chicken left in the village. There were still guns lying around in the woods that had been dropped by the retreating German army, and I had found and oiled a standard army rifle, a very dangerous undertaking. If we were caught with a weapon and reported, it was punishment by death or be sent to *Bautzen*, the internment camp. Few ever came back from there; they were starved to death. My father's cousin Willy, the father of Wilfrid of St-Michaelis who was a postmaster in Freiberg, was sent there and died within a year.

My father and I decided to shoot a deer in the forest. My father knew where they were. When we came close to where they were grazing, we heard a thump on the ground; the mother doe's warning that she had heard something strange. My father pointed to where the deer were, gave me the gun, and encouraged me to shoot. I was so surprised, I lifted the gun, took aim, and, as the deer started jumping off, my gun followed their jumps up and down but I could not pull the trigger. I froze. My father laughed and said it is quite common, but I felt stupid for letting the deer get away. A few days later my father went out alone, shot a deer, hid it in the woods, and came home to get me and a hand-pulled wagon. We found the deer, skinned it, cut it into pieces, and put it on the wagon under some old clothes to hide it. It was hard getting the wagon uphill in soft forest soil, and we both had to pull. We got home and put it into the cellar. However, coming out of the house, we noticed a trail of blood drops on the ground leading into the woods: a deadly giveaway. My father and I took some branches and pulled them over the trail of blood drops to wipe them out, doing it nonchalantly like gathering wood; it worked.

Another time when my father went out looking for deer, he came around a turn and suddenly there was a group of forest workers. He had his gun in his hands which meant a sure death for him if he had been reported. He started screaming, "Damn the guns, they are still lying everywhere, is the war not over?" and proceeded to hit the butt of the rifle against a tree until it broke. He must have looked so genuinely mad and against guns and war that the forest workers bought it. He was not reported.

The Russian soldiers came plundering nearly every day and took everything. We had no rights, and to this day I remember that feeling of total helplessness. Even when the Russian puppet regime, the East German Democratic Republic (which was not democratic but a Communist dictatorship that lasted until 1989) was formed, there was no protection for individuals under the law. If anyone denounced you as having said anything against the State, you would be deported, put in camps and, if you were lucky, come back after many years with a broken spirit and often broken health. Democracy, as imperfect as it can be, is far better than the helplessness we experienced then.

During these weeks following the end of the war, German refugees from Czechoslovakia fled across the border back into Germany because of the revenge killings by the Czechs of many thousands of Germans living in the *Sudetenland*. These were the days of starvation. I have a picture of my mother and father looking the size of 12-year-olds. It took three years until a limited food supply was restored. The black market flourished, and any valuables were traded for food. I saw a gold watch being traded for one loaf of bread—you could not eat the watch! The population became impoverished. The Russian soldiers stole what they could find. The ones from Mongolia were the worst, an uneducated lot that pissed into the washbasins and washed themselves in the toilet bowl. I saw one trading an armful of watches that did not work anymore—because he did not know they had to be wound up!—for one that worked. There was one boy in our village who could ride a bike freehand, an old bike put together with many parts. A Russian soldier came along on a good looking bike and saw the youngster. He traded the much better bike for the old one because it steered by itself. Of course he fell off and cursed, but by then the youngster with his new bike had gone.

The Russians started to dismantle the few factories still intact to ship them to Russia to rebuild their economy. They dismantled railroad tracks and shipped them east to replace the ones that were destroyed. For the next 45 years, the Soviet Union drained the few assets left in East Germany, yet the people survived with hard work and sometimes no hope. West Germany did not go through this drain. The Marshall Plan helped them get back on their feet early to establish a strong defense in Europe against the Communist East Block.

An optimist could say that lessons were learned from the Treaty of Versailles of 1919, that a country without hope will bring forth another demagogue, but I do not think so. For the Allies it was an act of self-preservation, a first line of defense against Communism. When I heard the West Germans complain about all the money they had to spend to get East Germany on its feet after the re-unification of the two Germanys in 1989, I had no sympathy. It was the East Germans who had, for 45 years, paid the bill for the West Germans to the Russian victors.

Chapter Fifteen

Back to Work—1945–46

In August 1945, things had settled down a bit and it was time to continue my hotel apprenticeship. As there were no hotels left in Dresden, I found employment at the big restaurant *Luisenhof* in the suburb of *Weisser Hirsch*. The restaurant was high above the Elbe River with a beautiful view over the valley and the city. It had two levels and could seat 400 guests. It had just opened again and as there were hardly any supplies, guests had to bring their own potatoes which were weighed and the equivalent weight served. Food was rationed: no stamps, no food. The beer was thin, but at least there was some. The garages had been requisitioned by Russian soldiers as a truck repair shop. It was very messy. I remember the German women lining up to prostitute themselves for a bit of food for their families. My bread ration was seven slices and had to last a week. Several times a week we got *Sandsuppe* for a meal: the floor sweepings of a flour mill. There were some flour and grains in it and a lot of sand that felt like grit on the bottom of the plate.

The black market took off; everyone traded something, with food the highest priority. We got to know the Russian mechanics and guards in the building. They were given "Occupation Marks" in denominations of 1000, 5000, and 10,000, and they had no idea of the value. We sometimes traded a bottle of wine for 5000 Marks. Compare this to a labourer's weekly take home pay of 150 Marks! As an apprentice, I received room and board and 150 Marks per month. Cigarettes were the currency: two cigarettes for a loaf of bread. I had made about 10,000 Marks in a short time and gave them to my father who repaid a mortgage with it to clear the title of the *Buschhaus*.

About four or five times a year, the Russians requisitioned the restaurant for a wild party that lasted three days: one day to prepare, one day to party, and one day to clean up. We collected cracked glasses from all over town because after the Russians gulped down a drink, they smashed the glasses, in true Russian fashion. As we had a few good ones left, we moved them out of harm's way so only old and cracked glasses were on the tables. The smell of roasted meat, good cooking, and baking filled the place, and we were very excited and happy, an opportunity to eat and steal anything we could get our hands on. We had no qualms; whole tortes disappeared, bottles of Vodka, anything. If we could not eat it ourselves, it was traded for durable goods that were later traded back for food.

These parties were only for officers of higher rank. About 20% of the officers were women, and some spoke German because of their Jewish background. They were often strapping types, well groomed. To enhance their figures in their uniform, they used bras with a kind of a stick under each breast to lift it up; they looked like two machine guns sticking out, with a large cleavage in between. I was serving *Eisbombe* at one of the parties, an ice cream cake with different flavoured layers. The guests were all drunk. As I served the ice cream to one officer, he jerked his arm up and tilted my platter, causing the ice cream to slide off and land directly into the cleavage of a female officer. I had immediate visions of being carted off to one of the camps, but luckily they all started laughing. The male officer put his hand down the cleavage, scooped up the ice cream, and slopped it on the table with loud laughter. I faded into the background with not even a smile.

A few days later I had a day off and visited my parents in the mountains, bringing some of the food I had stolen. They were happy to eat it, they were so thin. When I told the story they laughed, but immediately said that I was very lucky, because things could have turned very ugly.

It was a hard winter. My room was under the roof, and had no insulation or heat. The roof shingles had been rattled a great deal during the bombing the year before. One morning I woke up and there was snow on my bed covers because the wind had blown it into the cracks and it had settled onto the bed and floor. I got up quickly and went to work downstairs where it was warmer. I was determined to get out of this situation and vowed to never again be cold and hungry.

The Atlantic Hotel, Hamburg—1947

My apprenticeship was coming to an end. I passed my exam as *Hotelkaufman*, the hotel training needed to become a manager. As the facilities were very poor and the food very scarce, this training was limited. The best training I got was in survival. The director Bretschneider of the Bellevue Hotel where I started out had a daughter who was working at the reception desk of the Atlantic Hotel in Hamburg. I was introduced to her and she promised to help me with a job, if I could get there. The Atlantic was one of the finest hotels in Hamburg and was requisitioned as a British Officers' Club. This sounded like food and warm beds to me. My life in Dresden was going nowhere; the time had come to see the world.

The borders between the Russian Occupied Zone and the British Occupied Zone were very much controlled. The Russians did not want able-bodied men and women to leave the East because they needed the workers to produce the goods to be shipped to Russia. My father and mother agreed that I should go, although with a heavy heart. We did not know when we would see each other again, and the border crossing was dangerous. I packed a backpack and a small suitcase and off I went. My father gave me some last bit of advice on my way, the same advice my grandfather had given him some 50 years before: "Be honest, even if it hurts."

I had a square key that opened streetcar doors and also train doors. I had heard that Russian patrols checked the trains crossing the border to the West and removed able-bodied men and some women and put them in camps, to be reoriented to Socialism and then put to work. As we came close to the checkpoint, I took my square key and opened the door connecting the carriages. There was a lot of steam blowing from leaking pipes, which covered my presence. I then climbed under the gangway connecting the carriages and wedged myself into the wires and pipes close to the axle. I had an old army strap and used this to tie myself in as additional support in case I got tired holding on. The train stopped, the patrol came, the steam hissed, the patrol passed over my head to the next carriage, the train started to roll, and in a blink I was in the West. I scrambled out and went back into the carriage for my bags. Some people asked, "They did not get you?" and then told me of the others who had been removed.

I changed trains in Hanover and continued on to Hamburg. I walked from the station to the hotel on the banks of the Alster, a beautiful lake around which the city is built. There I found the staff entrance and presented my letter of introduction to Miss Bretschneider. She had prepared everything, bless her. I was shown a room under the roof with a bed and a cupboard. It was

warm! I smelled food! I started the next day as a commis, a waiter's assistant, responsible for getting the
things the guests order. My eyes popped when I saw all
the food. I was down to 90 pounds and hungry. The
first week I saved the scraps the guests left on their
plates and ate them, just to not to feel hungry any more.
The second week and later I only ate the leftovers from
the serving platters. I collected unused stale rolls from
the restaurant, dried them, and sent them home to my
parents to make soup. They appreciated it, and it helped
them to survive. Sometimes they traded some of these
dried rolls for other food. I sent them a parcel per week.
It was the beginning of my parcel supply that continued
for some 15 years, until there was enough food for them
to manage.

The population in Hamburg had little to eat. The
bread was made of maize or corn meal which was
rough on your throat. I was lucky being fed in the hotel,
as the occupation troops had all the supplies they needed. Since they were the occupiers, we had no qualms
about stealing whatever food we could. It was hard to
get it out of the hotel, but somehow we managed with a
friend watching and another dropping a package out of
a window when it was dark.

My school English was very limited and it took a
while until I could understand the British officers. One
asked me for an ash tray and I brought him some ice
cream! But in time it improved. I took language lessons
from a special teacher who spoke and taught eight languages. He had incredible patience and repeated each
word 10–15 times just to get the right sound. I took
Portuguese because I wanted to go to South America,
although I have now forgotten it since I did not use it. I
also took French because I would need it in the hotel
business. The pronunciation I learned from this excellent

teacher purged my German accent and I have often been taken for a native of another country when speaking French. My teacher moulded my pronunciation mechanism and ear until I could produce the sounds perfectly—showing that with effort and a good teacher, accents can be overcome. I also improved my German language. Coming from Saxony, I spoke the soft Saxon dialect and I became a laughing stock every time I opened my mouth. I was frustrated and spent many nights alone standing before the mirror, sometimes in tears, learning to open my mouth properly to produce the stiff High-German sounds.

I was then sent to work at the control office where the waiters' sales were checked and the money collected. They had a sweet deal going, as I soon found out. A waiter would order a tray of pastries and pay for it with a chit. He would tell my superior how many pastries were on the chit, giving my boss the chance to find the chit and destroy it. The waiter then sold the pastries for occupation currency, little bills of pence, shillings, and pounds, and these proceeds were split between the waiter and my boss. My boss then sent someone to the army stores to buy cigarettes for which you could trade everything on the black market. When we served our restaurant customers well, we received two or three cigarettes as a tip. In a week, I had 12–15 cigarettes saved up which I could trade for food to give to friends or send home.

On my days off, I often visited my sister Elfriede who lived in Winsen near Hamburg. She had difficulties finding food too, and my little bit helped. The trains were few and always packed. People were standing on the stepping boards beneath the doors, in between the carriages, and sitting on the roof. One time I returned from my sister's and had to stand outside the carriage on the foot board. The train had to cross the bridge over the Elbe near Hamburg. On the bridge the tracks are very close together to save space. Another train came from the opposite direction, and people standing on the foot boards had to make themselves as slim as possible. The other train's engine puffed by about 30 centimetres from my nose! Much too close!

One day a chef and three waiters from the hotel were hired to cater a private party in one of the beautiful villas along the Alster, the lake in the centre of Hamburg. We gladly did this extra work because we were paid in hard currency. The party was for 30 British officers and it started around 10 p.m. All went well, and at about 1 a.m. we were paid and sent home. On the way home I discovered I had left my silver cocktail shaker in the kitchen of the house and I went back to fetch it. I did not want to disturb anybody, so I sneaked into the door and into the unlit kitchen. I picked up my shaker and I glanced into the living room. The guests had all stripped naked and were frolicking to music in a conga line. Strange behaviour, I thought. When I joined my friends and told them, they laughed. "Stupid," they said. "Don't you know they are all gay?" I was so naive I had not realized.

My colleagues and I had had a few drinks, and pushed each other playfully as we walked back to the hotel. My nose came to my friend's fist or his fist came to my nose, there was a crunch, and my nose started bleeding badly. We got home and the bleeding stopped, but my nose was swollen for a few days. Fifty years later when I had a problem with snoring, a doctor tested the airflow through the nostrils and discovered that one of them was only 30% open. He asked me if my nose had ever been broken. I said no, but when he disagreed, I recalled that night in Hamburg. Fifty years later, my nose had to be reset to open the air passage. A few days after the operation, I could breathe much better. What a difference!

Visit to East Germany—1948

Currency reform: Each person could exchange 40 old Marks for 40 new ones. Overnight, all goods such as food and cars became available—you just had to have money to buy it. Commerce started to roll; new Marks were earned and spent. The West German economic wonder began. Christmas came and I had a week off and was homesick, so I decided to visit my parents. No problem with the train going east except that it was late and I did not arrive at home in the evening, as I had promised. A train delay made me miss the last connecting train out of Dresden and I could not get a lift. I found a barn, slept on the hay, ready to take the first train in the morning. There were daily shootings at the border, and my parents were very worried. My father said to my mother, "I'll find him." He went upstairs to a quiet room and concentrated in meditation. He told me later that he was able to follow my steps from when I had left the hotel in Hamburg until he traced me to the barn outside Dresden sleeping on hay. He came down and said, "Eberhart is all right, he will be home with the first train in the morning." And so I was.

When I arrived home, my father asked me how I had slept on the hay. I was surprised, how did he know? Then he told me the story of finding me. There are many things we do not know about. My father taught me to keep an open mind and to teach myself to use the subconscious mind. Even now, when I have a problem to which I do not know the answer, I tell myself before going to sleep that I will find the answer in the morning. Usually, the next morning when I shave or when I am in the shower, the answer pops into my mind. A direct message from the subconscious mind which had all night to think about it and come up with an answer!

We had a wonderful Christmas full of warm family feelings—Christmas carols, incense, and a little food. My parents were trying to get the *Buschhaus* going, but it was tough. The East German new Marks did not buy much. Their value was about four times less than the West German Mark. There were no supplies like soaps and linens, and customers had little money.

Then it was time to leave again, and with big hugs and well wishes I went on my way. The border crossings were perilous. The controls had been increased and nobody was allowed to escape to the West because the Russians wanted to keep all the workers in the East Zone. I took the train to Helmstedt, the last town on the line. Then, like many others, I walked toward the border. I had heard of guides who would take people across for a payment, and I had saved enough money for this. I joined a group of 15 people, including women with children, and we paid the guide. I knew the border was near a high voltage power line, so I became suspicious when the guide took us through the woods and declared after an hour that we were now across the border. Another young man and I told the group we would go ahead and scout. We walked briskly for about 20 minutes, and then the power line—the border—came into view. Suddenly we heard screams behind us: the main group had been caught. We ran under the power line and dove into the bushes on the other side. Shots rang out, and I felt a tug on my backpack—a bullet had hit my backpack and had shot a hole through my black pants which I needed for work. I have never forgiven the Russians for doing this. That was enough for me! I did not go home again for 16 years.

Baur au Lac Hotel, Switzerland—1949

I was now 19 years of age. Germany was divided between the East Block and the West, and the cities were still in shambles. There was no telling how long it would take for life to come back to normal, and anyway, what was normal? Looking back over the last 40 years, my parents had had a terrible time: the First World War in 1914, starvation 1918 to 1922, hyperinflation to 1925, then the "Gold Mark" when the new currency was pegged to the world gold standard—a great idea but nobody had any money—then the stock market crash in 1929. The failure of the Weimar Republic to establish democracy in Germany led to chaos and the rise of Adolf Hitler who came to power in 1933. He created jobs building roads and factories, and restored pride in the German people. The years 1936–1938 were the most "normal" years of my parents' life. Then Czechoslovakia was taken over and in 1939 WWII began. In 1945 the war was lost, starvation again, a country destroyed and divided. So in 1949, when I was in Hamburg, I decided that one member of our family had to get out of this mess of wars every 25 years and losing everything. I wanted to go to a peaceful country where I could raise a family without wars, where there would be enough food to live.

I could not go to England or France because there were no permits available and I also was concerned about their attitude toward a young German. Then Switzerland became a possibility. Mr. Geyer, the general manager of the Atlantic Hotel in Hamburg, had

English Girl,

German Boy

contacts at the Baur au Lac Hotel in Zurich, and he gave me a letter of recommendation. There was then and still is an international group of hotel managers who refer promising youngsters for training to leading hotels around the world. I·got the job and boarded the train for Zurich in the spring of 1949. What a change! In Switzerland, all the buildings were whole, the city was clean, and food was plenty. The scenery looking across Lake Zurich to the Alps was breathtaking. I was in heaven. We worked 12 hours a day during the main season, but it was worth it. I was paid very little, but it was the best life I had had so far. I saved up a few francs, and from the first month on I sent home a parcel every month with food, chocolates, coffee, and also cigarettes which my parents could use to trade for other goods.

This was the top class of the international hotel business, and the guests were wealthy and often famous since nobody else could afford such a hotel: European royalty, aristocracy, corporate managers, bankers and traders, famous artists, a who's who selection of the worlds wealthy and famous. There were very few Germans because they did not have the money. The British could only take a very limited amount of money out of Britain, but there were lots of Americans because the dollar was high. I started as a commis; assistant to a chef de rang, responsible for 4–5 tables in a restaurant. I had a lot to learn. The Swiss gave the Germans and the Italians the dirty jobs. They were so superior, calling me *Chaibe Sau Schwab*, stupid pig German. I developed a thick skin and swore to learn their dialect so well that they would accept me as one of them. After two and a half years in Switzerland, I was accepted as being Swiss. They thought I came from somewhere between Zurich and Basel, since no German could possibly speak *Switzerdeutsch* so well.

The first year I worked in the terrace restaurant was my real training in the top international hotel business. It was the first time since my training began in 1944 that everything was available for the guests: the best foods, the best wines, the best service, and guests from all over the world with a lot of money to spend. I learned how to make crêpes Suzette at the table and cerises flambé. Our maitre d'hotel, Mr. Guettinger, was a short, round faced, tough but fair man. He had a pot belly that stuck out at least a foot. He received the guests and seated them according to importance. He had an incredible memory for names, faces, and their preferences. He always addressed the ladies as madam, just in case it was not the wife of the man accompanying her. Years before, he had worked with Director Geyer, of the Atlantic hotel in Hamburg, at the Shepperd hotel in Cairo. Mr. Guettinger loved roast rack of lamb. He recommended it often. When guests ordered it and it was ready to be served, he was called to do the carving at the guests' table, which was always a ceremony with a good deal of showmanship to make the guests feel very special. This translated into good tips for him when they left. He usually planned to have a few ribs left over, which he then delighted in munching in his little office. One day four of us conspired to have the leftover ribs disappear. When Mr. Guettinger turned around for three seconds to face the clients, the ribs vanished. We had wrapped the ribs in a napkin and passed them down the line, onto a tray, and off they went. It went like clockwork. He was mad, trying to figure out how they could disappear so fast. His face became redder and redder, but the four of us stayed unfazed without moving a muscle. We felt sorry for him; we thought he would explode!

I had worked with the sous-chef de cuisine at the Bellevue in Dresden, Manfred Rytz, a Swiss who came to Germany in the late 1920s to work in a top hotel. After the firestorm of Dresden, where he lost his apartment, he moved back to Switzerland to Zurich. When I arrived in Switzerland, his wife, Alice, and her son Manfred became like a second family to me. I often visited them on my days off, and Alice was glad to wash my socks and look after my other clothes. To this day I call Zurich my second home. The first Christmas when the Rytz family had arrived back to Zurich from Germany, things were very lean for them. As new refugees they had very little. Manfred, three years older than me, carved two angels to hold two candles each, in the traditional *Erzgebirge* style. The Rytz family has all passed on, but I still have the angels 55 years later and they come out every Christmas.

The summer season came and the restaurant was moved out to the pavilion on the park overlooking the lake with a view of the Alps. Somehow they trusted me, and I took over a small bar to look after the guests who wanted to stay in the main lobby. This was not a hard job, but I had to be in control of things. Around the corner from the little bar were telephone booths for long distance calls. After a few minutes, the booths got hot and the callers opened the doors. Often the connections were bad and they had to talk louder and louder; I heard it all, and it opened another world. These guests were international traders who sold boatloads of fish from Norway to the USA, jute from India to Europe, oil, carpets, textiles, machinery, used planes, you name it. My wish to become an international businessman stems from these few months when I overheard these traders.

Autumn came and the Swiss government would not renew my visa. Their policy then was that foreign workers could not stay longer than one year as they would become too Swiss and the last thing they wanted was a lot of poor foreigners obtaining residency. For very wealthy foreigners, the policy was entirely different. They were welcome in Zug, Lugano, and Locarno, where they declared a negotiated income, much lower than the real income, and paid regular taxes thereon as an annual contribution to the canton's coffers. As this was a minute fraction of what they would have had to pay in their homeland, the number of luxury villas for foreigners on the side of the beautiful hills grew and grew.

Excelsior Hotel, Cologne—1950

I had to go back to Germany and got a job in Cologne at the Excelsior Hotel. The hotel was located just across from the famous Dome. The city had been badly bombed and rubble was still everywhere. It was October, grey clouds covered the sky, and it was wet, cold, and miserable. What a change from the beautiful and intact Zurich. I was there only two months, but it was enough to make up my mind to go to a country overseas which had been untouched by war.

Kulm Hotel, Switzerland—1951

At the beginning of December, I started work at the Kulm Hotel in Arosa, one of the best winter resorts in Switzerland. The team from the summer season at the Baur au Lac went for the winter season to the Kulm and I joined them. The Alps were breathtaking. We were 2000 metres high, nestled in a valley of chalets and rustic wooden Swiss farm huts. The international guests arrived with us and work started immediately, seven days a week and often 14 hours a day. The collection of international wealthy guests and their playgirls and playboys was colourful, to say the least—total decadence is more like it.

After a heavy snow, I was in the restaurant one morning and looked out at the mountain slope across the valley. I saw a small cloud of snow at the top that rapidly grew bigger and quickly engulfed half of the mountain slope. It was one of the biggest avalanches of that season. It was so fast I only heard the tremendous roar when it was almost down at the bottom of the valley. There were no casualties as the Swiss knew where the avalanches would come down and there were no houses or skiers in their path.

The food for the hotel staff was not very good. Swiss hotels know how to skimp on any expenses for staff. We had to wear white shirts and black tails for the dinner service. The black tails had pockets on the inside of the tails. If there were some leftovers from the platters used for serving the rich and colourful dishes, they were quickly wrapped in clean napkins and disappeared into those tail pockets. You just had to walk leaning back a bit so the loot would not bump against your legs. One evening a colleague of mine had a whole chicken left over and it quickly disappeared into the tail pocket. Only the headwaiter saw it. He called the chap over, took a gravy boat full of brown gravy, opened the top of the pocket and poured it in saying that, if my colleague wanted to enjoy the chicken, he might as well have some gravy with it. I never forgot my colleague's long face as he walked out of the dining room, leaning far back so the sauce would not drip onto his pants and into his shoes.

We were told we could stay one week after Easter when the hotel had closed for guests and have our holiday then. When the last guests left, our free week in the hotel started, including tickets to the ski lifts. I was in heaven. I rented some equipment and was on the slopes all day, every day. The run down from the *Hoernli*, a small horn on top of the mountain, was my favourite. One day I skied ahead of my friend and later he said I suddenly disappeared. The morning sun was blinding and I had not seen a cliff: I went over and looked around at what was happening as I had suddenly lost the ground. Below me was a deep slope of virgin powder snow. I had the presence of mind to turn my skis sideways as I fell into the deep powder, and it covered me up. My friend appeared on top of the cliff and saw a ski pole sticking out of the snow. Slowly my head appeared and I was laughing, having had such a wonderful drop into the fluffy powder snow. It took me a while to get back on my skis and we continued down; arms spread wide, flying into the valley. This was one of my best-ever skiing experiences.

I needed to stay a week in Germany before I could start the summer season again at the Baur au Lac. The Swiss authorities said this was my last visa extension. I wanted to go home so badly to visit my parents in the East Zone, but could not. Instead, I spent 10 days in Lindau at the Lake of Constance and in Bregenz, Austria, which was nearby. It was difficult to get a work permit again as I had already spent too much time in Switzerland. The hotel management successfully intervened with the authorities, but was told this was absolutely the last time my work permit would be renewed.

Preparing to Leave for Canada

I was now demi chef de rang, which is a junior chef de rang with a station in the restaurant, fully responsible for looking after the guests. It was an honour for me at my young age, and it also meant a few more francs which I could well use. My plans were firming up to go overseas to the USA; the trouble was a four-year waiting period as the quotas were full. One of my colleagues in the restaurant was Wally from Winnipeg, who was studying in Europe and working during the summer to earn some money. He told me about Canada, how big it was (he did not mention how cold), and how beautiful. That sounded good to me, and it was close enough to the USA which was my ultimate goal. I applied for Canada, got my visa, and then saved for the passage which I booked on the Homeland, leaving Hamburg November 1. I looked at the globe and found that the latitude of Montreal was the same as Venice and concluded the climate must be just fine.

Although I was a very late starter, I had had some romances before this last summer in Zurich. Then it hit me hard. Her name was Italina. She was from Venice, working at the hotel for the summer. She was two years younger, sweet with dark eyes and a beautiful smile. We were very much in love. It was a sad day when I had to board the train for Hamburg, not knowing when or if I would come back. We wrote to each other for years. However, time moves on and a long distance romance is hard to maintain.

Before I left Zurich I contracted with the Jelmoli department store to send monthly food parcels to my parents. I left them some money and later sent more from Canada. This arrangement lasted several years until the East German authorities forbade their citizens from receiving parcels sent by commercial enterprises.

Near Hamburg, I visited my sister who had just had a baby girl, Renate. Her in-laws and husband had just built a small house. There was little money, and the bricks were recovered from the rubble of the destroyed houses in Hamburg and hauled to the site. Building material was scrounged from here and there, but it was a roof over their heads. We had arranged for my parents to visit my sister, and for a few days we were a family again. My parents were so sweet and I loved them so much. They were always there when I needed them, giving me guidance and much love.

Chapter Sixteen

A New Life in Canada—1951

As I was leaving for another continent and we did not know when we would see each other again, this meeting had a special meaning for all of us. My parents and my sister brought me to the train station. When the train started moving, I looked out the window and there they were, waving goodbye with tears running down their cheeks, but happy for me as I was embarking on a new life. The train turned and they disappeared from my view. It was five years before I saw them again.

Good friends saw me off at the Hamburg harbour. The "Homeland" was moored at the pier, looking massive. My heart was heavy but also hopeful for a new life. It was part of my plan. One of our family should go to another continent where there was a chance to raise a new family in peace, not like Europe, which was still in ruins and had had wars every 25 years. The ship slowly floated down the Elbe river past *Blankenese* with the Suellberg restaurant on top of a hill overlooking the estuary. Not having much money, I had booked the cheapest passage on the boat, a cabin with two other young men at the stern of the ship just above the screw. After we passed the Channel we hit a storm in the Atlantic that lasted for six days. I was terribly seasick, and lying in bed was torture. The ship pounded into the waves, and when doing so the stern lifted into the air, causing the screw to spin around with a loud whine until it bashed again into the water with a thud. Sleep was impossible.

As we came closer to Halifax, the storm calmed and we could go on deck to walk around. On the passage I met an American girl, Rosemary Voss from Ocean City, New Jersey. She had been visiting relatives in Hamburg. She told me a lot about North America and taught me the currency: "This is a nickel, this is a dime, and this is a quarter." We had fun and kissed once just before the end of the trip. We wrote to each other for several years. After 13 days we finally arrived at the shore in Nova Scotia, heading for Halifax. I remember a clear evening gliding into Halifax harbour in calm waters. Buoys with their lights blinking guided the ship in. There were green and red lights, which meant a good omen to me: green for hope and red for love!

English Girl, German Boy

My New Life—1951

The morning of November 14, 1951 I got a stamp in my passport which made me a landed immigrant. The ship was full of immigrants, many with no money. I learned later that the "Homeland" made only one more trip and was then scrapped because of old age. We boarded an old train with wooden benches which had seen better days. The Canadian government had provided it for the immigrants. It rolled through endless forests, finally arriving in Quebec City where we were put into a camp surrounded by barbed wire for the night. Coming from East Germany, I had a distinct aversion to barbed wire. Early in the morning I went to the guard to ask why I was being detained. He asked if I had any money, and when I answered I had about $90, he said: "You are rich, you are free to go; this camp is only for those with no money."

I spruced myself up, took my letter of recommendation from the Baur au Lac, and walked up the hill to the Chateau Frontenac, the best and largest hotel east of Montreal. I was quickly told that the winter is a very slow time for business, long-term local employees had just been laid off, and there was no hope of a job for me. It was like a cold shower. However, I had another letter to Mr. Frossard, a Swiss, who was assistant manager of the Ritz Carlton Hotel in Montreal. I bought a train ticket, arrived in Montreal in the afternoon, and took a room in the Laurentian hotel where the tall IBM building presently stands. I had met some Canadian guys on the train who were jovial and laughed a lot. They came to the hotel lobby with me and asked me to come with them for a beer when I had checked in. As I was boarding the elevator to go up to my room, a clerk from the reception desk joined me and asked me if I had just arrived in Canada—I really must have looked like it! He asked how long I had known the fellows, and when I answered that I had only met them on the train, he told me to be very careful as many new immigrants had been taken out and robbed. I thanked him and stayed in my room. No doubt I was saved from big trouble.

The next morning I presented myself in the dining room of the Ritz Carlton hotel to speak with the maitre d'hotel who was a Danish man. He told me there were no jobs. I showed him my letter of recommendation to Mr. Frossard, the assistant manager, and I quickly sensed he was afraid of Mr. Frossard. He sent me upstairs to Mr. Frossard's office, who received me jovially, happy to hear from an old friend of the Baur au Lac. He said, "Go and see the maitre d'hotel and tell him to hire you, IF HE NEEDS SOMEONE!" I went down and gave the maitre d' Mr. Frossard's message, omitting the "if he needs someone" part. I sensed the tightness of the job market, and with my very limited resources I urgently needed food and shelter. The maitre d' frowned but said I could start the next morning. Hallelujah, I had a job! I found a room nearby for $6 per week, opened a bank account at the Royal Bank, and deposited my total cash reserve of $40. I still have the bankbook.

Everything was so new. I opened my eyes wide and listened to everything just to get my bearings. I had worked as a busboy before, and had more international experience than my co-workers. Six months later I had my own station in the restaurant, and a year later I became captain with four waiters under me. My career progressed well. But in those first few months I was very lonely. It took two weeks for letters to reach my parents. When the letters arrived, you could easily lift off the flap as they had been steamed open and read by the East German censors. We developed a family code, and in time we could say a lot to each other without the censors getting a hint. I have kept all the letters from my parents from 1951 until they passed away in the early seventies.

My dear, dear Eberhart,

The white powder snow is falling quietly transforming the world into a wonderland. I am thinking back 21 years ago when you arrived. What a pleasure you have been to us. You have within yourself the faith, the love, and the light which grew within you when you were a child. May it guide you well in your beautiful new future. Whenever I arrived at a crossroad or I was in a "low" I went into the forest or into a church to find the way to continue...

People are gathering pine cones and selling them for 10 Marks for 50 kg to make some extra money. The mine in Altenberg is going full blast with 3 shifts. (This is the Russian plan to extract all the precious metals from German mines as part of the war reparations. They are after tin, wolfram, and bismuth for steel hardening, molybdenum, etc.)...

Your loving father.

English
Girl,

German
Boy

My dear, dear boy of my heart,

...for a long time I was very sad after we waved good bye to you at the train station. All my best wishes go with you. You are going so far and over the great ocean. When will we see each other again...

I have cut a sheet of air mail paper in quarters because I have to write a bit more but do not want to use a whole page as this would increase the weight of the letter and postage is so expensive...

With much love and hugs,

your mother.

Then Christmas came. I put three little angels from the *Erzgebirge* on top of my Phillips radio and decorated with two little Christmas tree twigs; this was my little corner of home. All the festive spirit, the anticipation of Santa Claus, the smells of the incense, the tingling of the bells, all was there on this little radio. I looked at it often and played back in my mind the happy days of my childhood. On New Year's Eve the celebrations at the Ritz Carlton Hotel went into the early morning, helping me forget that I was alone in a big new country. Some comfort came from a family living in Montreal on De Bullion Street, a relatively poor neighbourhood. I had been introduced to them by Manfred Rytz, my best friend from Zurich. They were poor people, but had golden hearts. They were the first people in Canada who cared for me, and they helped me a lot.

Besides the loneliness of those first few months in Montreal, there was another problem which weighed heavily on me. It was the fact that I was German. The war and the post-war years were full of stories of atrocities committed by Germans. The newspapers and television had daily reports about how bad the Germans were. Almost every movie coming out of Hollywood referred to the bad Germans. It was an endless deluge that was to last over 50 years. It affected me so much that when someone asked me where I came from, I answered Switzerland, which was true, but not the right answer. I remembered how we were told in school that we were the greatest young people with a wonderful future ahead of us. The German achievements in literature, music, medicine, science, technology (over 50% of all world patents before 1939 came from Germany), archaeology, and art proved that we were an intelligent people. However, after the war ended in 1945, survival was the daily necessity. When I went to Switzerland in 1949, I experienced the first wave of anti-German sentiments. But now in Canada, alone and feeling full-blown prejudice, it made me withdraw into myself. I was not bad like everyone told me I was. I had done nothing wrong, neither had my father nor my grandfather. This burden of collective guilt of all Germans was hammered home daily wherever I turned. It weighed heavily on me. I felt as if I were floating in a vacuum without any footings or support. I was in agony drifting into space. Who was I?

In this agony I found God. I had been baptized a Lutheran and received confirmation at 13 years of age, but rarely went to church. The church of our family was the forest, the mountains, and the soft valleys with the clear water running in the creeks—nature. Now, alone in Montreal, I went to the United Church in Westmount. The singing of hymns and the sermons gave me such comfort that I began going regularly to the service. There I met some people that belonged to the Moral Rearmament Association. They had a vision of a better world without corruption and wars. They believed in me and told me that I was good and had many good things to do in my life. I talked to them often and they invited me to their houses for meetings. Over the next years, they and the church gave me a chance to find a new footing on which to stand, giving me comfort and strength to carry on in spite of the burden of the collective German guilt which relentlessly appeared in the media.

Meanwhile, my parents carried on running the *Buschhaus* through the difficult years. In 1943 it had become an army hospital; in 1945 it was free and business could continue—or could it? There was very little food, no material to keep the house in repair, and hardly any coal to heat it in the freezing winter when the central heating pipes froze and often burst. The Communist government continued squeezing the last bit out of free enterprise. They even nationalized my uncle's bake shop because he had two helpers working for him. He was then hired back as manager, put on a salary, and worked 10 hours a day starting at 8 a.m. How stupid that was. When he was self-employed, he worked 14 hours a day, got up at 4 a.m. to bake fresh bread and rolls for the store to open at 6 a.m. After he became state-employed, he got up at 8 a.m., which meant no more fresh rolls or bread early in the morning for the town. Nobody said anything, because if you spoke negatively about the system, you were in trouble or disappeared.

Times were very difficult for my parents. They were then both 63 years old and had worked hard all their lives. My mother wrote to me in December 1951 just after I had arrived in Montreal.

My dear Eberhart,

I wanted to write to you about something. Some time ago, I believe from Hamburg, you sent home a pair of used boots. I have no boots for the winter and I was wondering if you would mind if I use them. We have no money available before the Christmas season to buy some. I tried them on and with a few extra pairs of socks they fit. You would make me very happy if I could wear them, they even look smart.

Your father still has the boots you bought for him a few years ago. With the money you gave me I have bought some wool and have knitted 3 pairs of socks. I will give them to him at Christmas. He will be very happy.

Your mother

I also received letters from my father indicating that my sister was having a very difficult life. I read the letters and I knew things were not right in my sister's house, but I was much too young and naive and could not understand the severity of it all. My sister married in the last days before the end of the war with the Russians advancing. The age group of men from which she would normally find a husband was about 75% decimated by the war, and those that were left were mostly injured, had lost arms or legs, and were often so damaged psychologically that they did not last long. All of this played a part in her marrying when she did. She wanted to get to the West. However, the marriage was a mistake, and she suffered greatly. She had to live with her in-laws: he smoked like a chimney and she was neurotic, totally dominating, and gave Elfriede no chance to develop herself. She was a serf in the house. By 1951 she had three children, with no help from their father, and all the burdens of a horrible mother-in-law. I have always advised our daughters and granddaughters to learn a trade or study a profession so they can be independent and support themselves and their family. I never want them to become so dependent on their husbands that they have to suffer abuses as my sister did.

In 1951 my father wrote:

...I have to write Werner (Elfriede's husband). There have to be changes. The situation is so destructive, the young family has no chance to grow. The children are totally dominated by the grandparents, they have no chance to develop themselves properly, and Elfriede is too tired to fight it every day without the support of her husband, who is on a ship 11 months at a time.

But what could he do? He was behind the Iron Curtain, could not visit her freely, and had no money to help. The exchange rate was 5 Eastmarks for 1 Westmark, and anyway, he did not have any Eastmarks. He could not ask her to come home because the East Zone was hopeless. It was a very difficult and painful situation that lasted many, many years.

Settling In—1952

In March 1952 in Montreal, I saved up a few dollars and bought myself a pair of skis and a jacket and warm gloves. On my next day off I took the bus to Ste. Adele. I walked to the bottom of hill 40/80, took the lift up, and standing at the top I saw the beautiful scenery of the Laurentian Mountains, the town, and the frozen lake. Together with the smell of cold forest air, I was in heaven. It was just like home. I promised myself that I would always ski and be close to nature. I felt good: I had a new beginning, a new job, enough money to buy skis, and now a trip to enjoy nature.

In the spring I was promoted from busboy to waiter. My good training in Switzerland gave me the edge. I learned English and French whenever I could. It was not long before I felt comfortable enough in both languages so I could make myself understood and follow conversations. In the summer I took up tennis and played at the McGill grounds on Sherbrooke St. and University St. in the afternoons between the lunch and evening shift. What a feeling it was—to have arrived! Several times a week I took courses at McGill University in accounting, feeling it necessary to improve myself. I wrote letters to my parents and my sister weekly, and they replied as often as possible.

....here is a contact address in West Berlin where I will be in 3 weeks. You can send a letter there. (My father was visiting in West Berlin. There he could write a free letter without the risk of censorship. But, just in case this letter did fall into the wrong hands, he gives a wrong sender, he calls himself Paula, and as address, the town of Misery Nr. 2.)

...we have enough to live on, rape seed oil, 6 sacks of wheat, potatoes, and our goat is fat. His name is Max, he comes to me when I call him...I have asked that the (party) meetings be moved to the Forsthaus. This way I am less involved and do not know everything...The taxes for the August quarter were almost 3000 Marks, how can we pay that much...Let us thank God that we are all healthy.

With greetings from my deep, deep heart,

Your father

A New Car—1953

About this time I met Peter Nickels, who had just arrived from Rostock, East Germany, via Hamburg. He was to become my best friend for the next 50 years.

I had saved a few dollars and really wanted a car. I bought a 1950 British-made Ford Prefect, lime green in colour. It had not been used much and still smelled like a new car. It had a small engine with four cylinders the size of a shot glass. The top speed was 50 mph, but I felt like a king. In the afternoon between shifts, I polished and waxed the *green beauty* with great love. Of course we horsed around with it too, and once stuffed 12 people in it, albeit with some legs and arms stuck out the windows. My first long trip was to Niagara Falls on highway Nr.2 along the St. Lawrence River. From Toronto to Niagara Falls it was called the Queen Elizabeth Way, a double highway. I put-putted along the side of the road, when suddenly my car was pushed onto the shoulder of the highway. It took all my presence to control the car when I saw a bus disappearing in the distance. The air pressure from the fast-passing bus had almost pushed my little car into the ditch!

On June 17 there was a demonstration in Berlin, a people's uprising. The Soviets brutally used tanks against the demonstrators who only wanted to improve their lives. After this, my father did not want to continue his membership in the Unity party. He had joined the Social Democrats in 1947. Two years later the Communist Party, fully supported by the Soviets, forced an amalgamation of the Social Democrats with their Communist Party and called it the Unity party. It was a forced takeover, and this is how my father became a member of the ruling Communist Unity party. He could not stay in a party which supported the bloody Soviet oppression of the demonstrators in Berlin on June 17. But how could he get out? Resigning would send a signal to the authorities that he was against the system, and that had deadly consequences. Instead, he gave his reason for resigning as: "I cannot condone the SLOW progress of Socialism in our country." The authorities could not say anything against his reasoning. However, they knew what he was thinking and, from then on, tried to break him economically with extra taxes, forcing him to give service to mean functionaries sent as guests to squeeze and threaten. There were terrible scenes where they threatened to throw him out and confiscate the property. He was helpless against the Regime. All the time he was hoping that somehow things would turn around, however they did not during his lifetime. I did not know much of this then, as he had no way to describe it in the censored mail. My father also did not want to burden me with the full details. So it was only bit by bit and many years later that I pieced things together.

My cousin Helga Troeger fled to the British Zone just after the end of the war. In August 1953 she visited her parents and brother in Geising, East Germany. My father asked her to write an uncensored letter to me after her return the West.

We visited the Buschhaus. They have a lot of work, 70–80 persons for meals and your mother works so hard, she has only one person in the kitchen to help her. Socialism allows the help to work only 8 hours per day and holidays can be taken in the middle of the high season—the owner can do nothing!

It must have been much worse before June 17th when nationalization was in full swing and a flood of refugees arrived in the west. June 17 was the day of the uprising in Berlin when demonstrations took place against the Communist regime. The population was fed up. This breath of freedom was quickly and very bloodily squashed by Russian tanks. Many died. (There were no more demonstrations for 36 years, until 1989.)

Private businesses are charged with huge taxes they can never pay. Their income is kept very low. Your father told me that he has to take guests from the Labor Union. They pay 2.80 Marks per day per person and for this he has to provide accommodation and three meals a day. They are being bled white. Anyway your father was quite entertaining. He stood behind the bar in the evening and started singing one folk song after another, and the whole restaurant joined in...

Many regards,

Helga

My parents continued to write letters to me.

...But my dear Eberhart, when you go hunting and there are bears in the forest you must be very, very careful. If a bear gets wounded it can turn on the hunters and tear them apart, like lions and tigers do sometimes to their keepers in the zoo. Please watch out...I have sent to you a small parcel for your birthday, it is only 6 handkerchiefs and a twig from the tree in front of the house. I wanted to keep it small to be able to send it by airmail. It was only 850 grams. When I came to the post office they wanted to charge 105. Marks. I could not afford that much, so I sent it to you by regular mail (ship) which will take 3-4 weeks. But you know it is on the way...

Your loving Mother

...When you shoot a bear you have to know the anatomy. Where to aim when he is facing you or when he is turning away from you. Use a strong gun and strong shells! Watch out! Last evening we heard a very strong stag roaring in the woods near us and another stag, just as strong challenging him on the other side of the valley. They roared so loud the trees seemed to vibrate...

Father

...We are so glad our help is back. She had three weeks of holidays. We had to do all the work by ourselves. I was so tired that when I sat down for a minute I just fell asleep. My back is often in pain, rheumatoid arthritis, the doctor said. I have to get injections every 4 weeks. Thank you for sending the medicine... M

...We just received your parcel. What a joy. Real coffee, chocolate and cacao. We had a feast...M

...Thank you for your postcard of Montreal. I counted 20 floors on the tall (Sun Life) building. It would make me dizzy looking down from it. Your description of the trip to the country was great. Of course it is much nicer with a girl friend. I well understand, I was young once too! But do NOT bind yourself too early. Enjoy your youth, it comes but once! I am so looking forward to seeing you again, who knows when. May God be with you and protect you.

Your Mother

...We had a lot of guests New Years Eve—worked to 5:30 am with Vatel and one waitress. But I had to get up at 6:45 to prepare breakfast. Only 1.15 hrs sleep—that was not enough at my age of 65. But these holidays are always a lot of work and we cannot get any help when we most need them...

M.

I sent a letter to Thiessen Dairy Products in Schleswig Holstein, with whom my grandfather and father had dealt before the war:

I remember well the weekly packages which arrived from you and which I was allowed to unpack as a boy...Times have changed. I am now in Montreal, and I want to send regular packages of butter to my mother. She is a pensioner and can receive them without duty. Please do not use printed material or addresses of your company; it has to look like "family" mail. I enclose US $10, approx. 42. West marks. Please establish an account for me and I will send parcels regularly...

..We just got another parcel from you, such delicious contents. I love a cup of real coffee in the afternoon to pick me up when I am tired. We now only have 55 guests; for the last months it was 75–80 per meal and often parties in the evenings. We had so much to do that I did not have time to write...I miss you so much, when will we see you again?? Vatel bought a new motorcycle, an EMW. It looks beautiful and even has a passenger seat...We went for a test ride, it's so great (age 65). We are thinking of riding it to Elfriede but it would take 2 full days of 8 hours each to get to Hamburg. We cannot do it before Oct. 15th because we cannot close up and by then it may be too cold...I am glad you decided to wait for a while to find a wife. You still have lots of time...

Your mother

...You have now been in Montreal for 2 years. How do you feel about your work and career? Have you seen any other directions you may wish to go? The first one does not necessarily have to be the best one.

How soft are you with your girl friends? Are they robbing you of your youth? From what family and educational background are they? Are they looking for house and home? Do you share costs?

I would like to remind you that you, like I did, have met people who have abused their youth and now have to live their life as HALF persons. You are alone in your new country——only a healthy body will give you the energy you need to compete successfully. Do you have a place where you have some peace so you can look within yourself to find new directions and inner clarity?

I now have to climb on the roof and shovel off the heavy snow...

Your father

...I have just started firing up the central heating. 50 kg briquettes cost 3.50 Marks. How can I keep the whole house heated 24 hours per day? We just cannot earn enough to pay such prices. We are short of cash on all fronts but hope to coast until the Christmas season when we are booked full until March.

If you could have Detlefsen in Denmark send me two parcels with 9 pounds of butter each, to our name, not the business address, then I could return the butter to the people who lent it to me...

Your father

...We heard that the second parcel you sent to us by the company in Zurich was confiscated because commercial parcels are now disallowed. Only private parcels from person to person are allowed. Now we will have to use Elfriede as sender.

...soon it will be Christmas. I think you will have a lot of work and not much time to think about being all alone so far from home...but within yourself you will always have your belief, the light and the love with which you grew up as a little boy...

...you have a great opportunity to plan and work for your career. Plan the different stages carefully and set your goals. You are a hard worker and will get there...In due course you will find a girl with whom to share your life. Take your time, build your future first and then the right partner will come along.

Meeting Tessa—1954

Spring came quickly in Montreal. One week there was ice and snow, and the next green grass. Guenther, a colleague of mine, asked me to join him and his girlfriend for coffee and cake at the Pam Pam coffee house on Stanley Street. Many new immigrants met in the coffee houses on Stanley Street just below Sherbrooke. Guenther's girlfriend brought along a friend. They both worked at the Gazette newspaper. She was a little shy, but had a beautiful smile, and we talked about many things. I was not only attracted to her physically but also to her intellect. She had something to say about everything—and she still does! Her name was Tessa.

Tessa and I met soon again and we walked up to Westmount Mountain, talking about everything. We took a rest on the little bench below the lookout. The scenery was breathtaking. The city was below us and in the background the mighty St. Lawrence River. We saw each other as often as we could, but being almost five years older, I had more things in mind than talking and kissing! Tessa was a strong Catholic with firm convictions. The mother of Luise, Guenther's girlfriend who had introduced us, was a practical French Canadian also with strong Catholic convictions. When she heard the four of us planned a day trip to the Laurentians, she told Tessa, "You can do anything but do NOT take your pants off." Well, she didn't! Soon after that my interest faded and we split up. Tessa returned to Quebec and wrote poetic letters to me for a while, but then they stopped. I did not know that she had gone to England. I began a new romance with a Spanish girl who also worked in the hotel. I still thought of marriage sometime in the future, but was not ready to settle down yet.

English Girl,

German Boy

My job at the Ritz Carlton Hotel in Montreal went well. As waiter, I was in charge of four tables in the dining room and was soon promoted to captain with three waiters under me and twelve tables to look after. I took the orders from the customers, recommended the special dishes, and made sure all was served properly and on time. This position gave me an opportunity to talk to people and make them feel happy with the service and the meal. I must have done well because soon some of the regular guests asked especially for tables in my section. This did not go unnoticed to the management, and the following season I was promoted to be one of the captains in the night club. Work started at 5 p.m. and I came home to my room at about 3 a.m., stinking of smoke.

I did this job for two years, and then the head-waiter job became vacant in the Maritime Bar, one of Montreal's high society hangouts at that time. I had European waiters and we gave the guests the top service I had learned in Switzerland, doubling sales in one year. We were popular, and I had the courage to ask the Director of the Hotel for a raise. The waiters were getting the tips and I picked up a few dollars here and there, but had a very small salary of $150.00 per month. I asked for $30.00 more. When there was no increase on the next payday, I quit, arrogant enough to show them that I meant it! However, it did not matter to them a bit because every month boatloads of immigrants landed in Montreal, and there were plenty of trained people who did not dare ask for more money.

Nov. 7, 1954

Soon you will start your second 25 years. You are so far from us but we feel as if you were in Dresden. We are very close to you in our spirit...Remember when in 1948 you came home from Hamburg for Christmas? There were a lot of shootings at the border and in the evening, when you did not arrive with the last train...We were so worried. I went deep into myself in prayer and meditation. I was able to follow your progress from Hamburg step by step until I found you in Dohna, sleeping in a barn. A calmness came over me; I said to your mother "He is fine, he will be here in the morning." You even arrived earlier than I thought the next morning, as you had jumped off the slowly uphill moving train in the Mende-forest and took a shortcut home...We were so happy...

Your loving father

...events moved quickly. As of Dec 15. 1954 we will lease the Buschhaus to a younger couple. They will pay us a small rent but we are still responsible for repairs. This is difficult to calculate how much these repairs will cost, but the laws are such that there is no other way for us to retire. (The repairs proved to be more than the rent received; this way the Government made sure that private enterprise died out.)

You have to always be a nose length ahead of events. Your mother has worked so hard all her life it is amazing how much she has done. The last day we just finished dinner for 40 guests, when 2 buses arrived with 80 more guests. We all quietly pulled together, prepared and served dinner with a smile. The guests remarked upon the good food and the efficient service. They did not know that this was our LAST PERFORMANCE...

Your father

(Pensioners over 65 years of age got permits to visit family in West Germany. If they did not return to the East it did not matter, as old people were only a liability to the state. My parents wrote this letter from the West, without the risk of censorship.)

December 21

...we just arrived in the West at Elfriede's house and will stay the holidays. It was so good to see her and the children...Renate age 5 said: Grossmutti, I want you to stay like you are now and never get wrinkles...

Mother

...All people connected with the Berlin Uprising in 1953 have been arrested and nobody has heard from them again. It is terrible how most people now walk around with their head down and when they talk, they look behind them first to make sure nobody is listening. I cancelled my membership of the Unity Party because I could not be part of a party, which caused the brutal destruction of the demonstrators in Berlin who only wanted more to eat and freedom. My reason for resigning was: I could not approve of the SLOW progress of Socialism! I was lucky, it was accepted. If they only knew...

Your father

New Career—1955

I had been lonely at times during those first four years in Montreal. One of the problems was the shift work in the hotel business and not having any weekends off like everyone else. I also started to think of planning for a family: life alone was not what I wanted. How could I have a decent family life working every evening and weekends and having only one day off during the week? I decided the time had come to change careers. I had a German friend, Klaus Lada, who worked in the real estate business. I asked him about real estate, and decided to give it a try.

Klaus worked at a real estate office on Guy and St. Catharine. They hired me. I was shown a desk and a telephone which I had to share with Klaus, and I was told to call people to ask if they wanted to sell their house. After a few days I found one, and someone in the office came with me to ask the right questions to list it. It was a little veteran's house on Hampton Ave. in NDG opposite the tennis courts, worth $8,500. A few weeks later I sold it, and my new career was launched. From May to December I earned $900 in commissions. As this was not enough to sustain myself, I answered an ad for salesmen selling food plans. Food I knew, but what was a food plan? I soon learned that it was really selling freezers with wholesale food in them. The buyers ordered the cheaper food every month, and they added the payments for the freezer to the monthly food payments. This way they could pay it off over two years. I could do this job in the evening, and after a bit of training, I sold 2–3 plans per week. After 6 months, I bought myself a new car. Things were looking up.

Back to Germany—1956

Spring came and with it the decision to find a German girl to marry. The trouble was, there were no German girls in Canada. Parents in Germany let the boys go to a foreign country so far way, but not the girls. I wrote my sister in Winsen, near Hamburg, asking her to please find some girls for me to meet and that I would visit her in four weeks. I was ready—like in the supermarket—to pick one off the shelves. The most modern plane then was the Constellation, a four-motor

propeller aircraft which took 14 hours from Montreal to
Frankfurt with a fuel stop in Gander.

I had not seen my parents for five years and so
longed to be with them again. They could not come to
Hamburg as there were no permits available right then.
Instead, we planned to meet in Berlin. They could travel
to East Berlin and then take the subway to West Berlin.
There we had a friend who had been helping get
parcels and money from me to my parents. We decided
I would fly from Frankfurt to West Berlin, avoiding the
border controls, and meet them at our friend's house on
a certain day and time. I was about an hour late when I
arrived in the dingy postwar Berlin street, looking for
the number of the house where we had planned to
meet. As I came closer, I saw my parents just leaving the
house, walking in the other direction. They had not
seen me. There they were, arm in arm, walking slowly,
a little more bent over, chatting. They were sad that I
was not there—I felt it. I loved them so much. For a
minute I walked behind them, getting closer. Then I
blew our family whistle—da dee da—the one we used
as children when picking mushrooms in the deep
woods. They froze, turned around, and then both their
arms flew into the air and we hugged and hugged all
three together. What a happy welcome. Four great days
followed, and then it was time to leave again.

My next stop was Hamburg at my sister's and
her four little children. Over the next week I met the eli-
gible girls my sister had picked out for me. I was determined to find a wife, however it was not successful: one
was too big, much too big; another was too aggressive;
one's parents' were too anxious (I heard them tell her to
move closer to me on the sofa because "he will take
you to Canada"); another had nothing to say, no opin-
ions about anything; and so on. After ten days I gave up

English Girl, German Boy

and returned to Canada without a bride, my head hanging low. It was a sad time in my life. Little did I know that it would take only a few months more to find the love of my life!

Marrying Tessa

One day, I received a telephone call, "Hello, this is Tessa." I answered, "Tessa who?"

"Remember we met four years ago?" Then the penny dropped. We chatted, and I asked her out for dinner to Desjardin's Famous Seafood Restaurant. I was very pleasantly surprised. Tessa had grown into a beautiful young lady with a charming smile. Two days later I invited her to visit some friends who had a cabin in the Laurentians. We had a few drinks, and that night I proposed. Three months later we were married, and 9 months and 2 weeks later our first child arrived.

Tessa was still Catholic, and as a Lutheran, her church would not accept me and marry us unless I signed that our children would be brought up Catholic. I reasoned it out this way: Protestants and Catholics have the same God. How can He not want two people who love each other to marry? These restrictions are man-made. I signed the agreement with the understanding that the children would be educated Catholic but would also know about other religions and that, when they are old enough, they can choose whatever religion they want. It worked. ·

Weeks before the wedding day, on a sunny afternoon, Tessa and I visited the top of Westmount Mountain. The view over the city and the St. Lawrence River was breathtaking. I laid out my plans for the future. We would get married, have a large family, Tessa

English
Girl,

German
Boy

would stay home to bring up the children. I would give my full commitment to the family and work very hard to provide for them. And that is what we did. It was much simpler in those days than it is now. With love, we overcame our different backgrounds. We simply lifted ourselves up to a higher level; the century-old German–English prejudices just could not touch us.

It was hard work, but there was also success and recognition. I took real estate degrees at university, later formed my own corporation, and became a successful international broker placing European investors' funds into North American revenue properties and managing investors' portfolios. I was a founding member of the German Canadian Chamber of Commerce, and later was elected President of the Montreal Real Estate Board which had 6000 members. I also developed and built multi-million dollar residential and industrial projects in Montreal, Toronto, Winnipeg, and Vancouver.

We had five children and now have eleven grandchildren, and there may even be a few more in the future. While Tessa stayed at home, she earned two university degrees and was an active volunteer. She was on the board of directors of both The Junior League of Montreal and Les Grands Ballets Canadiens in her role as publicity chairman for both organizations. At the time of writing, we have been married 48 good years and there are still many chapters to be written about the rest of our story which will come later.

To show how hate and wars can be overcome, we decided to write this book for our children, grandchildren, and future descendants.

Part Three
Return to Germany

Dresden 1979.
The Frauenkirche
(Church of Our Lady)
still in ruins 34 years after
the end of World War II.
It was totally reconstructed
by 2005

Chapter Seventeen

Germany During the Communist Era

All of our children and most of our grandchildren have visited both Coventry and Dresden. They saw the bombed-out landmarks of old Dresden before reconstruction, and they experienced Communism in the old East Germany when we spent Christmas there in 1979. They have seen the Berlin Wall, passed through Checkpoint Charlie, and returned in 1990 to a united Germany.

Martin made two escapes from Communist East Germany, the first in 1947 and the second in 1948. After his second escape, he decided it was too risky to go back again. It was not until 1964 that he dared to return. By this time he had a Canadian passport and felt reasonably safe. We took three of our four children with us, the youngest only six weeks old. Tessa had had a Caesarean section, so was still feeling rather fragile. Our oldest two children were four and six years old. She decided to go by boat to England with friends to make the journey more relaxing, and then meet Martin. Peggy, her mother, was naturally full of misgivings and felt sure she would never see us again.

The year 1964 was the height of the Communist era in Germany. We were searched thoroughly at Checkpoint Charlie and crossed through the Berlin Wall into a grey, dismal land. The Wall had been constructed in 1961 to keep East Germans from fleeing to the West. Early on the morning of August 13, 1961, the German Democratic Republic (GDR/East Germany) blocked off East Berlin with barbed wire and antitank obstacles.

Tanks gathered at crucial places. The subway and local railway services between East and West Berlin were interrupted. Inhabitants of East Berlin and the GDR were no longer allowed to enter West Berlin, among them 6,000 commuters who had worked in West Berlin. A solid wall soon replaced the provisional barriers. It was 3.6 metres high and stretched for 166 kilometres. We were surprised the Wall was so low and seemingly non-threatening. After August 23, 1961, citizens of West Berlin were no longer allowed to enter East Berlin. The forced evacuation of houses situated at the border of West Berlin began. The GDR propaganda called the Wall an "anti-fascist protection wall." Hundreds were machine-gunned to death as they desperately tried to escape.

As we drove from Berlin to Dresden, we passed watchtowers manned by soldiers with machine guns, colourless villages with dilapidated or abandoned houses and farms. There were very few cars, but the tiny funny-looking Trabant (Trabi) ruled the road. It was as if time had stood still as we watched the people in their drab clothing shuffling along the bleak streets, eyes fixed to the pavement, not daring to look up. We had made an effort to bring our shabbiest looking clothes, trying not to look conspicuous. There were severe food shortages so we brought along suitcases loaded with goodies for Martin's parents and relatives.

Martin's parents' hotel had been confiscated by the Communists and was filled with workers spending their holidays. We stayed in Cousin Kate's guest house next door which seemed trapped in a time warp. The walls had not seen new paint in 50 years; the toilet was a bench with a hole in it. The only source of heat was the ofen, a tiled sort of stove which warmed one room but left the rest of the house cold. The house had three floors and 14 guest rooms and looked like it had seen better days. Cousin Kate's father was a violinist and a direct descendant of the composer Robert Schumann.

We visited another cousin and his family who had a very large farm. They were known as "capitalists" in their village and so had to share their impressive three-storey house with workers. They were allowed one floor for their own use. While we were visiting, Martin's cousin closed all the windows so that eavesdroppers could not hear our conversation as we murmured in low tones. Spying on neighbours reached epidemic proportions during that time, and people were hauled off to jail on any pretext. Everyone suspected everyone.

Dresden, previously the "Florence of the north" and one of the most beautiful cities in Europe, had been devastated by the allied bombings. The Russians purposely left the ruins to remind the German people of the horrors of WWII. They built ugly, square boxes and called them apartments—gone was the graceful architecture of prewar Dresden. The Opera House and the Frauenkirche were still in ruins. Everything was grey and monotonous, just like the food.

1979

In December 1979, we visited East Germany for the second time. The Russians invaded Afghanistan at this time. We took all our children with us, the oldest 19 and the youngest 9. At that time, it was unthinkable that, in 10 years time, there would be a free East Germany. In fact, the Communist iron fist seemed stronger than ever. We spent Christmas in the mountains at Cousin Kate's house. The highlight of the holiday was a New Year's Eve party at the family's hotel next door. There was dancing and folklore singing and the place was filled with Communist party members. They all wore the party badge in their lapels. Of course, we were a curiosity even though we tried to make ourselves melt in.

Tessa remembers dancing with one particular man who actually said he could stop us leaving the country if he wanted to because they still considered Martin to be East German, even though he had a Canadian passport. It was rather worrying, but Tessa decided to keep her head down rather than get involved in a discussion. We had invited a couple of Martin's young cousins who lived in Dresden. They were in their twenties, handsome young men with absolutely no future ahead of them. They wanted to see our passports. They looked longingly at them and said, "We can never have one of those and we can certainly never go to Canada." At this time East Germans could only travel to other Communist countries and certainly not to the West. They were trapped by history and circumstance for 28 years.

Our children were incredibly touched by their cousins' fate. They started scheming all sorts of ways we could smuggle them out of the country, somehow hiding them in our Volkswagen bus. But they decided it would not work because the cousins were well over six feet tall and rather difficult to hide! At Checkpoint Charlie they examined our bus underneath with mirrors, along with every inch of it, so it would be suicide to try and smuggle them out. At that time, the television was full of news reports about the mighty Russian army's march into Afghanistan.

Buschhaus 1979.
Martin, Tessa and family
celebrating New Year's.

Our Children's Memories
Heidi

Our children could not believe that people could live with so little freedom and felt genuinely sorry for the trapped people imprisoned in an unforgiving ideology. Heidi is our eldest child and has very clear memories of our trips to Germany.

My earliest memory of East Germany was when I was four years old. I remember it being a wonderful visit with warm people. I remember leaving East Germany and going through Czechoslovakia, where we got stopped at the border for several hours. I understood that Dad was not going to be allowed to leave because they thought he was maybe Martin Bormann (Hitler's deputy), and they were checking his passport. Although he had a Canadian passport, his birthplace was Germany. This was the first that I learned of the Nazis, and my first association with them was therefore fear. I remember having nightmares about the Nazis coming and invading our house and taking us away. It felt like I had one or two of these nightmares every week and, as I got older they reduced in frequency, but were always terrifying.

For me, World War II and its aftermath were always present in my life. I would say that it has only been since the Wall came down that this has lessened. Growing up, I read every book I could get on World War II and life in Communist countries: The Diary of Anne Frank, *historical novels, and hundreds of spy novels. War* movies (yes, including The Sound of Music) and stories of amazing escapes and defections from behind the Iron Curtain were a staple.

In university I studied sociology, abnormal psychology, and behavioural psychology, and always at the back of my mind I tried to get some understanding of how people could possess the oppressive and cruel mentality that both Nazis and Communists had, or how they could rationalize their behaviour. I also tried to understand how people managed to survive war, conditions of war, and the atrocities that they endured. I tried to understand what motivated people to get up every morning, when that meant that they would be consciously enduring oppression. At least asleep, I reasoned, one could escape in dreams.

I felt incredibly lucky that I was not living behind the Iron Curtain or in wartime England or Germany. I also felt guilty because I was lucky. On some level, reading about the survival stories helped me cope with that guilt. People were surviving without my help, and that helped me to feel less responsible for entire countries. I wanted to do more to help our family behind the Iron Curtain. I would fantasize about developing escape plans and helping them settle in Canada. I was so happy that my father's sister Elfriede was in the West and that her kids were in the West. I could not understand why my grandparents Grossmuti and Grossvati chose to stay in the East. I now know that they had pensions and so had to stay there. I just wanted them to be free.

Up until I was nine or 10, my brother Martin and I played war games with the other kids in the neighborhood, not cowboys and Indians. We even had little cap guns to shoot at each other. Martin and I were always on the same side, and we had to rescue each other when taken prisoner. I don't remember who won, because the game would invariably end when it was time for dinner.

In 1969 we went to Austria and England. In Austria, I can remember going through a pedestrian tunnel under a street and there being an alarm on the inside of the tunnel wall. Martin told me that if we pressed it, the police would come, and they were German police, so they were very scary. I was totally mesmerized by this alarm button, and as everyone walked ahead, I stood there staring at it, until I pressed it. I still don't know why I pressed it, but I did. Immediately the alarm went off, and the police sirens wailed. I ran absolutely terrified to catch up with everyone else as I heard police boots running behind me. I really thought my nightmares had come true! They never did find out who pressed the alarm button, and we calmly walked away. We saw Grossmuti and Grossvati in Austria, and they seemed to be fine. My frustration at the time was that I could not communicate with them directly because I could not speak German. There were so many things I wanted to discuss with them and I couldn't say anything.

The next time I went into East Germany, it was 1979 and I was 19. By this time, I had had a steady diet of books, movies, study at university and school, and still had Nazi nightmares about once a month. Although not fluent, I could speak enough German to get by. We were there at Christmas and politically the situation was tense because the USSR had just entered Afghanistan. I felt extremely rich and Western—trendy clothes, sheepskin jacket, warm winter boots, and a body shape consistent with a balanced diet which did not rely heavily on starch and potatoes. Dad had told us to be careful what we said to people because we were being watched. Although I was still afraid of Communist police, I trusted our relatives and spoke openly with them in safe places. It was very sad to hear how everything was a struggle because the government basically took everything away.

For me, as a top competitive swimmer on the national level, the treatment of athletes—the elitism, the performance enhancing drugs, and then the rejection they experienced when they were used up and no longer at the top—made a massive impression. I had been competing against these people, and I had been competing for fun and love of the sport, not for survival like they were. Again, I felt very privileged and a little guilty because of it, but also tremendous pride and appreciation of the enormity of what Dad had accomplished: his escape, his moving to a new country and learning a new language, and then creating his own success in business. I stopped feeling guilty because I realized feeling guilty was undermining his accomplishments. I was relieved to leave East Germany, but I didn't realize how stressful it had been for Dad until he let out a huge whoop as we passed through the border.

In 1984, I returned again to East Germany, this time just with Dad so that he could attend a school reunion. I spoke even more German this time, and found it to be a fascinating place. The people struck me as being so creative, inventive and resilient, and I felt that they could do anything they wanted. I felt that if I were the government, I would be very afraid that these people would overturn me. I did not realize at the time that this was exactly what was happening. There was a tangible difference in the mood of the place from 1979 when people were genuinely afraid of being arrested. In 1984, they spoke much more openly about their escape plans, criticizing the government, black-market trade, and underground activities. I felt they had been galvanized into action, and it was exciting. I enjoyed the people for who they were and got to know them well, even in a short time. Dad was much more relaxed during that visit.

In 1986, Cousin Kate came to visit us in Calgary. By that time my first child Matthew was a one year old, and I was delighted to have her stay with us. For me, this was my contribution to showing her what life was like outside the East. I wanted to show her everything, so she could understand what our life was like. I was astounded when shopping malls overwhelmed her. We had to leave Toys R Us because she felt sick at the sheer volume of toys and consumerism. She kept saying "Who needs all of these toys?" In her eyes, all of this was excess and wasteful, and irrelevant to what was important in life. She much preferred the scenery and nature, and we concentrated on that. As a young married person with a little one, I was very much in that phase of working to acquire items, and her reaction to this was a reminder to me about the important things in life. She was quite happy to return back to the East, knowing that her needs were met there, her roots were there, and she was comfortable there. I understood then why people stayed in the East even when they had the opportunity to leave.

In 1989, the Wall came down. I was glued to the coverage on TV. In 1990, all our family and grandchildren visited Prague and East Germany. I was struck on that visit by how arbitrary the whole forty years of oppression had been. Before the Wall came down, the guard towers on the border were my nightmares come true. On this visit, they were abandoned, overgrown and all but falling down. It felt wonderful to cross over into the East and be free. People were happy about the Wall coming down, but also uncertain. Like Kate, they had been socialized and almost institutionalized in some ways. My friend Vera told me there were big problems with parenting. Before, the state had provided daycare for workers' babies, and those children literally stayed in care through school until they were adults. Suddenly parents had to cope with raising their own children without the State there for assistance. Vera told me that many of her friends had no idea how to parent their kids. She chose to move to the West, and her husband and children stayed behind in the East. She still has this arrangement 15 years later. Her husband was never able to adjust to life in the West, whereas she and the kids have.

It sounds as if the German side of the war impacted me much more than the British side. This is not true—it is simply that for me, the British experience finished when World War II finished, and they rebuilt their country and their lives. The German story continued much longer than that, and into my life experience, because for me the war only ended in 1989 when the Wall came down. I know the challenges there continue, but now they feel self-imposed.

Growing up, we used to joke about World War II continuing in our house because we had a parent from each "side." However, I never did feel that any war was raging in our house. And for me, being half British and half German was fine. Growing up as a competitive swimmer and representing Canada in competitions, my allegiance was firmly with Canada, not with Britain or Germany. I was and still am proud of my British and German heritage, but I am and remain Canadian.

We blended our British and German heritage and traditions so well, that it was only when I spent Christmas in Germany that I realized which traditions were actually German. For me, passing on these traditions, especially at Christmas, is really passing on a family tradition rather than a British, German, or Canadian

English
Girl,

German
Boy

tradition. I don't remember any anti-German feeling when I was growing up in Montreal. Even discussing the war in history class, I did not feel aligned with one side or the other, and nobody treated me as a German, even with the name Heidi. I was proud to tell the story of how both sides of my family coped with the war. I think because Dad escaped, and had told us those stories of defying the Nazi regime and also the Communists, I was classified as coming from a family that resisted the Nazis and Communists, and therefore I was respected as being almost one of the "underground." The fact also that my mother's father Jack died in the war, and the effect that had on my mother and her family, brought home the fact that I was also British. I was seen as the first genera-tion of two refugee parents who were both victims of that war.

The only time I remember any anti-German feel-ing while I was growing up was from my British relatives. My British grandmother (Welsh actually) was openly hos-tile toward my father, and indeed toward anything German. I suppose on some level that was understand-able, given my grandfather's death. But I could never fig-ure out why she continued to feel this way toward my father since he had been too young to fight for the Nazis, and his family had resisted the Nazi party.

My mother's sister and her children were very quick to pronounce me "German." They would not nor could not fathom that I was also part British. They used to call me a Nazi, and then when I told them they were too ignorant and stupid to worry about, they started call-ing me a Yankee. I told them there was no point trying to explain the difference between Canada and the US and just grit my teeth. They seem to have grown out of all of that now.

• • •

I did go to Coventry, and I remember a town with a big church. The age of buildings and structures in the UK still strikes me as amazing. To me, the bombing of Coventry was really a small piece in the history of Britain. It felt like a very small snippet when you could also see Stonehenge and Roman viaducts and 1000-year-old farmhouses. I later read the book Sarum which was a history of England and again was struck by how awesome the history is there. I am afraid the bombing of Coventry faded somewhat in the context of the history of the area.

I felt the same thing about Dresden. Buildings there were also centuries-old, and there was always the feeling that the area would be able to recover, just because it always had before. I think the firebombing of Dresden had more impact on me as an event because my father told us of his experience and showed us where the hotel had been standing and where he was rescued by his father on the riverbank. We saw evidence of the bombed Frauenkirche which looked as if it had been bombed yesterday because nothing had been cleaned up or restored. In contrast, Coventry had recovered and become a vibrant city again by the time I saw it, reinforcing its resilience.

The fact that Dresden feels like a living history to me is reinforced by having married my British husband Jonathan. His father Jack was one of the bombers of Dresden. I hold no ill will against him; he was seventeen years old at the time and doing what he was trained to do. I think every British and German family will have some story about their involvement in World War II, and unless their politics today are objectionable, I feel I can-

not hold their family history against them.

Since my mother's stepfather was the only grand-father that I knew really well, his fighting in World War II with the Royal Rifles of Canada was also significant to me. When I see or hear about World War II, I identify mostly with Canada, Britain, and the "underground" Germans. Remembrance Day for me feels like a bringing together of all these histories; I never feel divided. Instead, I feel that the losses on all sides of the war are remem-bered. I feel that Remembrance Day is there to remind us that war is never the best solution, and peacefully resolv-ing conflict is always the better path. Remembrance Day is about the grief that all sides felt in all wars, not just World War II.

Hollywood is still making movies about World War II and I think the movies being made now are much more balanced than older ones. You actually see now that there were many Germans against Hitler and the Nazis, and it explores their powerlessness at being able to do anything to stop them. I think the idea of methodically and systematically killing millions of people because of their religion, colour, and lifestyle choices was so incon-ceivable that many people lived in denial. I think this is more about the human condition than about one coun-try. Since that time, war atrocities have continued and although people know or suspect it might be happening, they feel powerless to do anything to stop it. Who knows? In a hundred years George W. Bush may go down as a great leader of his time because he was willing to go against public opinion to try to stop atrocities in Iraq. The whole oil story may get left behind.

Megan

Unbeknownst to us, our third child, Megan, wrote a journal while we were in East Germany in 1979 and smuggled it back over the border to West Germany. She was 17.

East Germany

Dec 24, 1979

I haven't been able to get paper, so I'm behind schedule. This is the only paper I have (Kate gave it to me) so I have to use it sparingly. On December 20, 1979, we flew from Montreal-Amsterdam-Hamburg. We were all dead-tired from the trip when we arrived at my father's sister Elfriede's in Winsen—about an hour out of Hamburg. She was very obliging as usual. We saw our cousins, Wolfgang, Renate, and Helmut, Sabine, Michael, Peter, Ingrid. We had a great time—just spent the night. Then we drove for about 9 hours to get to East Germany (DDR). We crossed the border at a town called Helmstedt. Oh! By the way, we are traveling in a VW bus beige/brown. The memories!! The border was patrolled by DDR soldiers who believe in Communism. The border was very crowded. It took us about 1_ hours to go through. There were lookout towers, barbed wire, high walls, there was a bit in between BRD (Bundes Republik Deutschland—West Germany) and DDR (Deutsche Demokratische Republik—East Germany) called no-man's land. The soldiers were very mean looking but turned out to be very nice. They were joking around and stuff. They didn't search our car. Daddy was so nervous before we crossed; he was screaming and snapping people's heads off! Once we passed the border we went past Berlin and Dresden to Hirschsprung. Ah! What can I say about Hirschsprung! It is a tiny village of 150 people. Very old. We are staying in Haus Charlotte, *cousin Kate's mother's name. She died a year ago. It's a guest house. Very cozy.* Ofens, *large oven-like tiled furnaces using coal.*

We went to a tiny church, the smallest I've ever been in, for Xmas eve service, Lutheran, the nativity play—very modern, moral. "They can take everything else away but they can't take Christmas" referring to political situation. Although Daddy told us to keep quiet about politics, there is quite a bit of political conversation. The minister we had was a political prisoner during the war. His sermon was on the religious crisis in the world. We visited Dad's cousin Walter in Geising. It was there that I found out just by experiencing, what the DDR people are like. His wife Regina, (amazing woman), at age 15 was dragged off to Siberia, USSR and stayed there for 12 years. During that time she was raped and sent back because she was pregnant. As a result she had a daughter called Vera, 19 yrs.—a really nice girl—and a son by Walter, Gerhardt, 16 years old. The most charming, obliging, down-to earth, pure, honest, loving people I've ever met. So different from people in England summer 1979. Don't know what BDR people are like, but have heard they are not so friendly. DDR people stare at VW bus because it is from the BDR, but wave anyway. There is so little, but so much. No fakeness or superficiality. No impression has to be made, just themselves. They've told us so many stories I can't remember them all. Kate is a wonderful person.

Had Christmas Eve party at Haus Charlotte. *Another cousin, Walter Tröger's family, came. Gerhardt* was Santa, lots of presents, Regina amazed by Polaroid and candy canes.

December 25, 1979

Woke up late, 11:30. D's great cousin Ellen Schaal, Grosvati's cousin Trudy Borman, and Herr Kunitz stayed for a while. Then went to visit Mrs. Ritz who was staying at a friend's house in Dresden. The Fischer's (friend) were good people, very hospitable. Went to Seligen house, Ritz's niece to see her ceramics. Beautiful! Husband professor of astronomy researching sun flares. Went back to Fischer's and had dinner. Watched Xmas celebrations on TV. All I do is eat, sleep, and listen to German. Mrs. Ritz was speaking French v. hard to adjust. She can get me a family in Switzerland where I can be an au pair girl. Nice to see her again. Went for a night walk. D. told more stories. Love it here. I forgot to say, less than 1/2 pound of coffee is 20$. Cocoa worse, 40$, ordinary pair of shoes 100$, 1 BRD mark=4 DDR marks. It takes 2 years until you can get a TV. Costs $4,000.

Dec.26

Went into Dresden looked at some buildings, went to Albertinum Museum, beautiful! Everything from classical art to jewelry. Diamonds! Rubies! Sapphires! By the millions! Saw some ruins, very sad. Dresden was Florence of the North before it was bombed. All old buildings black with soot. Mrs. Ritz came with us and met Frank Fischer, Mrs. R's nephew. Had lunch at Luisenhof Hotel on top of mountain overlooking Elbe. Dad worked there when he was 17 as an apprentice. Saw his tiny office. Great lunch! Mrs. R and Frank went home. Went to visit D's great-niece Renate and husband Egon. They joined us for a musical concert (classical). We were stared at because we were in pants. Renate called it a fashion show. Styles are so behind the West, the women wore long patterned dresses, patent leather shoes, and homemade white wool crochet shawls. 60's style! Very interesting. Everywhere we go we are stared at!

Dec 27

Went to Meißen. China factory was closed. Went to see huge castle Albrechtsburg, very nice. Meißen wasn't bombed but houses were falling apart because no one can afford to repair them. Very sad to see old buildings go. Kate came with us. Went to see D's cousin Elfriede Philip (originally Börner). They live in a small part of their big old house that was taken away from them. Eat! Eat! Eat! Billboards all over the place about the good of socialism. People are so humble. Once again like England '79 we saw the name Borner inside of Meissen Castle. Crest was gold lion on black.

Dec.28

I still have not been able to buy paper. It's a good thing D. bought some new shirts! (At this point I was writing on the cardboard insert for shirt packaging.) *Got up early and went to Zwinger, a gorgeous museum. Half Baroque style and half neo-renaissance. Started building in 18th century, it houses the work of well-known Dresden artists. Italian, French, Czech, Russian. Rubens. Fantastic. The Zwinger was damaged (bombs) but some has been reconstructed. Herr Kunitz came with us as our cultural guide, a great gentleman. Met Cousin Rainer, Renate and Egon's son. V. good looking. Heidi took a liking!!! Had lunch/dinner nearby. D. showed us where his hotel was that burned down, and showed us where he escaped the fire bombs during Dresden fire bombing by the*

British and Americans. Saw Augustus the Strong's castle, church and mistress' house. He had 365 kids. Then went to see D's Cousin Charlotte Schenk, Grosmutti's niece. Has bad arthritis. V. nice old lady. She has to wait 10 years to get into a nursing home. It takes 12 years to get a car and 10 years to get a telephone. Terrible!!! We were going to go to the operetta but Mummy was sick, immer krank!! *Everyday we are tired—it's terrible. We do so much everyday. Still no snow. Costs 20 pfennig to take a crap and 10 to wash your hands! Saw Börner name again – Felix Borner – a porcelain painter.*

Dec.29

Got up early. Heidi, D and I went into Dresden. H and I wanted to shop but found out no stores were open. Dad had hassles at bank, couldn't take all money out. Then went inside August the Strong's church, gorgeous! Beautiful altar and organ. Then went to see D's Cousin Walter Kempe in Hainsberg, didn't stay long. Bought much needed fruit. Jeans cost around 100$! Hil, Heidi, Dad and I went to folk singing get together at night in a town nearby. D. knew the hostess, old school mates. Mum was sick, didn't go. Then went to a dance in village nearby. Modern dancing. Met Vera, Gerhardt, Hans, his brother and wife Elke. Dancing was fun, D taught me new steps. Was asked to dance by a party member!!!!!!!! Said yes. Didn't know he was Communist till after. Vera told me to speak "many English." He didn't understand a word I said!!! I found out he was married and had 4 kids. I told him I was too and had 5 kids!!!! He believed me. He was drunk. When he got too close I said " Mein Mann ist hier" *and he backed off. Guess he thought I wasn't so young and fresh after all. It was very interesting and fun. Elke was telling us what it was like in Russia. It was a fun night!*

Dec. 30

Went to Grosmutti's and Grosvati's grave, Kate's mother's too. Put some flowers down and had a moment of remembrance. Graves are in Altenberg. Then went to great cousin Wilfred Börner about 1 1/2 hours out of Hirschsprung. Fantastic farm, 6,000 pigs!!! All mechanically fed and germ free. The organization was amazing. Every pig was biologically known from snout to tail. He won many prizes for his pigs. Was once all his own, but now owned by the state, and he gets a salary. He works very hard. There is such frustration everywhere. People are never left free without remembering what situation they are in. Very little pleasures left to be enjoyed and the get togethers that are, cannot be sometimes trusted. This extreme is so hard on people. We had a snowstorm overnight and Kate's prediction came true, we have snow before the New Year. Everything looks so much more friendly with snow...It looks like Hirschsprung!!

Dec.31, 1979

Jesus Christ, what an emotional night!!!! I've never been sadder about leaving a place than I have leaving here. The people envy you because you're from a free country, but not in a mean way, but in an amazing way that a free country like Canada exists. I feel so sad to leave the people when all I have given them is just the concept of freedom not the actual dream of it. How these bloody Russians can say that this kind of government is successful, I don't know. They (USSR) seem to be so sure of themselves, but I know there's a fault somewhere, and sooner or later it will fall. We have seen Communist groups who live in GBR and come to DDR for holidays. How can they be so hypocritical!!!!!!!!

We went to the Buschhaus *for Sylvester (New Year's). It is so well taken care of. I'm so happy it is. The manager (Haus is owned by state) squeezed D in for tickets because he had heard so much about the Family Börner that he had to meet them (meaning my grandparents owning the house before it was taken away by the Communists). He was a very nice man and I danced with him although he could not waltz. People there could tell we were from Canada and you could see the questions in their eyes about what freedom is like. Especially the teenagers that were there. There was one man friend of Kate's who gave Mummy a napkin with the words on it saying "Great freedom of Canada! Happy New Year!" and other things. He asked Mummy to dance and when he was dancing he said to her, "You come here and give us freedom but when you go you take it with you." And he said, "1980 is a new year there are changes for you, but for us there are no changes, no improvement." So sad. When we said good night to the guests in the Haus Charlotte, who I haven't even met but they were so friendly, I had to close the glass door between the dining room and the hall. I turned back and they were waving, I waved back, it was like shutting them out from the world or at least from me. Isolated. Cut off and they still waved with tears in their eyes. One lady didn't want us to leave. This trip has been so overpowering and intense that my brain is all sapped up. I have absorbed and learnt so much. What the world is made of is shit!!!!*

Jan.1, 1980

Had to leave Kate today and go to West Berlin. She was crying and got teary-eyed. I really like her, she's so sweet. So we left snow muffled Hirschprung, went through East Berlin where we had a fancy lunch. We used Grosmutti's and Grosvati's account money. So it was a special meal, very tasty. Went through Checkpoint Charlie were thoroughly searched, I was glad I hid my notes. D asked me if I had torn up my notes and got rid of them, I said yes. He was really nervous about getting into any trouble, but I was sure that my notes would be ok in my pants...I kind of feel bad about lying to him, and I was scared when we went through. All the guards look so threatening. The actual point was sort of like a maze. With cement blocks, wire, gates, lights. All the houses on the point were abandoned. There was a full moon and it did look very creepy. What a difference from East to West Berlin although West Berlin is just an island in a sea of communism. More lights, cars, noise, ads, flashy shops, big company buildings. Really different. So much better taken care of. Beautiful apt. houses, and there are definite social classes. Went wandering all over W. Berlin to find hotel. D was our "Joseph"! Found Hotel Am Studio. Very clean and nice. As long as there was a bed, bath, H20 we were eternally grateful.

Jan. 2, 1980

Charlottenburg Schloss *was a castle we went to in West Berlin. Was lived in by Friedrich the Great and other kings. Gorgeous palace everything was gilded, artwork and furniture beautiful. Went to "The" Wall at many points: 1) the Hall of Justice; 2) the Brandenburg Tor; 3) Checkpoint Charlie. Took tons of pictures. The wall itself is so measly, but it's what is around it. Guards, lights, wire, mazes. Kufurstendamm is a famous street we saw in Berlin. Shops galore! Saw victory column. Also went into a tiny one room museum about Checkpoint Charlie and the history of the wall. Fantastic, just amazing what DDR people went through. We got a book about all the escapes and so on, fascinating. Then D hurried us off to Winsen where Elfriede lives. It took about 5 hours. Glad* to go to bed. *All the guards were joking around and very friendly. Disappointed at the meanness of the guards. Thought they were mean. Saw the barracks where thousands of USSR soldiers live and train. Arrived at Elfriede's to a feast fit for a king, ate then conked out. Going home tomorrow.*

Hilary

Hilary is our fourth child and was a six-week-old baby when we took her on our first visit to East Germany in 1964. Here is what she remembers of later visits.

My first clear memory of East Germany is Christmas 1979 when we embarked on a family trip to my father's birthplace, the village of Hirschsprung (Valley of the Jumping Deer) near Dresden. I was 15 years old. It was the first time we travelled to East Germany "en famille." I felt a mixture of excitement and nervousness because we had heard stories of people who were shot as they were trying to escape over the Wall. I was worried that my father could be arrested, despite the fact that he held a Canadian passport. As on my father's previous trips to East Germany, we loaded up suitcases with goodies that were a luxury: coffee, cocoa, sugar, salt, tea, and other staples that were nearly impossible to get. I remember thinking what a treat it would be for our East German family!

Despite the hardships, everybody welcomed us everywhere we went. The return of the prodigal son, my father, was a joyous occasion! They welcomed news of the West and loved our treats. I have distinct memories of two cousins: Rainer and Vera. Vera was the daughter of my father's cousin's Baltic German wife, Regina, who was deported to Siberia as a teenager and was raped there by the Russians. Vera was the result. She was beautiful and I was particularly impressed by her colouring: blonde, blue eyes, and flushed cheeks. Later, I learned that her cheeks were permanently flushed because of exposure to severe cold when she was a baby in the deportation camp in Siberia. Rainer was about 20 and was the son of another cousin. He was strikingly handsome, tall, blond, and blue-eyed. He talked about his dream of going to the West, still an impossible dream in 1979. We discussed the possibility of hiding him in the car when we left, but quickly realized it was much too dangerous. We knew that cars were fully inspected, which included looking for hidden seats and other secret compartments. It was simply too risky.

Dresden had not changed since the end of the war. It was still a city of ruins including the Frauenkirche and the Semper Opera House. It was hard to believe that Dresden was once the pearl and cultural centre of Europe. We visited the site of the hotel where my father had worked to inspect an iron door in the embankment of the Elbe River. It was here my father escaped from the devastating allied bombing and where his father found him and took him home. We walked through the forest in Hirschsprung where I was indeed treated to a jumping deer crossing my path! My father spent many hours with his father learning which mushrooms were edible and which were poisonous, knowledge he passed on to his children.

* * *

Despite the lack of many things we took for granted, tables were laden with plenty of food and some of the best Kuchen ever! After enjoying much feasting and Christmas cheer, we headed back to the West. It was difficult to say good-bye. This was the Cold War and the future was very uncertain.

On our journey back we visited an elderly aunt of my father's in Dresden. She lived on the top floor of a walk-up that had not seen any renovations or upgrades since before the war. She was so gnarled with arthritis; I could not fathom her going up and down the steep stairs. When we left, she insisted on seeing us to the front door and I remember asking my father how she would get back up on her own. He said not to worry; going up is easier than going down!

We then travelled over the border at Checkpoint Charlie to West Berlin where we visited the museum devoted to the Berlin Wall. I was fascinated with the ingenious methods people used to cross to the West: tunnels, remodeled cars, suitcases, and many more. German engineering at its best! Of course, there were also tales of unsuccessful attempts and the sheer waste of young lives was difficult to understand.

The two Berlins were as different as black and white. West Berlin was busy with shoppers and the stores full of Christmas trinkets and toys. East Berlin, on the other hand, was devoid of any of these luxuries. The buildings in West Berlin were modern and well-maintained, but in the East they were ghosts of the past. The Wall itself was an imposing structure. It must have been difficult for each side to see the other, one flourishing and one stagnant.

When we left East Germany in 1979, I had not really thought it would be possible to return. We certainly did not expect the Wall to come down only 10 years later! We did manage another trip "en famille" in the summer of 1990. In addition to the four children, we had four grandchildren (plus one in utero) and spouses. We were a group of 11 and travelled in two vans. Of course, the first difference was not having to pass through a check-point any longer. The family in East Germany was still as welcoming as ever, and optimistic about the future. Buildings had improved and the city of Dresden was undergoing renovations—the Frauenkirche was hidden under layers of scaffolding!

One notable change was the busloads of tourists. We visited the famous Meissen china factory which was buzzing with tourists. Capitalism had clearly arrived!

Jason

Our youngest son Jason also has memories of trips to Germany as a child.

I was nine years old the first time I went with my family to East Germany. I had heard many stories growing up and was a little concerned about what it would be like to visit a Communist country. I remember packing suitcases with all sorts of goods that were unavailable or simply too expensive for my father's family. I always thought it was odd to take women's stockings to a country that was lacking in other essential items!

I remember crossing into East Germany at Checkpoint Charlie, which was easier than I thought. I later learned that entering the country is not the problem; leaving is another matter. It was Christmas, and I remember celebrating New Year's Eve at our old family inn. We set off fire crackers which was the first time I had ever played with them and thought it was great! Christmas trees were decorated with real candles instead of electric lights. The pungent odour of incense burning from Rauchermaenner, small wooden carvings of folkloric figures which puffed out smoke, the smell of coal burning stoves, the Stollen Christmas cake, and the spiced wine will always be Christmas for me. In Canada we continued many of the same traditions and, for me, Christmas is not the same without them.

At the New Year's Eve party, my mother talked with someone about the situation in East Germany and the longing he had to escape to the West. Even a simple conversation like this was dangerous during those times. The ever-present possibility that someone in the room was a Stasi informer kept people looking over their shoulders. The Stasis were East Germany's secret police. After the Wall fell, it was discovered that one in five people were part of the Stasi secret police or were working as informants, so the fear was justified. The man my mother spoke to wrote a note to her explaining his desire to leave East Germany and come with us. My mother, ever the journalist, wanted to bring the note back with her to Canada but my father said no, took the note, and tore it up into pieces. But my mother was not to be stopped, and she took the pieces and hid them in her suitcase, unbeknownst to my father!

We left my father's village on our way back to the
West and once again stopped at Checkpoint Charlie. We
lined up with other cars to pass through, but my father
was nervous so we were all on edge. East German soldiers were all over the place with big machine guns and
scary looking faces. Guard towers were also manned
with snipers ready to shoot anyone trying to cross the
impossible gauntlet of barbed wire, mines, attack dogs,
and a huge wall. In the midst of all this was our
Canadian family in a red VW bus with a father holding
a Canadian passport stating he was born in East
Germany. We came to the first guard booth where they
took our passports and put them in a small capsule which
was vacuumed into some far away building for inspec-
tion. Then gruff guards in imposing uniforms swarmed
over the car with mirrors to look underneath, opened our
luggage, tapped, poked, and smelled their way around
our car for what seemed like an eternity. Even longer
and more agonizing was the wait for our passports. I
remember my father getting nervous, and I can't imagine
what my mother was thinking about the note somewhere
in her suitcase. If the guards had found it, they would
have had reason to keep us there and who knows what
could have happened. Finally, we were given our papers
back and waved on, zigzagging our way through the
tank barriers down the last stretch to the West. Then and
every other time that I crossed the border I felt as if the
guards were just waiting for something to happen—a
twitch of the wheel, driving too fast, driving too slowly. It
was an eerie feeling which evaporated as we drove past
the sign "Welcome to West Berlin"!

When we returned to Canada my father was
furious with my mother for smuggling the note out, and I
remember we kids talking about it all. I thought it was
great that my mother had the nerve to get the note out as

a symbol of our trip and a way to explain how hard life was for East Germans then. I don't know how I would have felt if we had all been thrown in jail though!

After the Wall came down, I had many conversations (which usually turned into arguments) about German reunification with German friends my age. West Germans seem to feel cheated because they took on the burdens of the East which resulted in a deterioration in their lifestyles. They see East Germans as lazy and uneducated and have a real prejudice towards them. I always come back to the point that it was a united Germany that followed Adolf Hitler on his crazed adventure across Europe, and a united Germany that was responsible for the Holocaust. It was only the decision of the conquering powers which sliced up the spoils of war into what became two Germanys: the East Germans just happened to be on the wrong side of the thin red line.

The Russians were very eager to punish the Germans for the 20 million deaths they suffered and treated East Germany accordingly. The West meanwhile had no reparations to make. When my generation talks about being upset with reunification, the loss of their lifestyle and economic success, it really makes me angry. Look how much an entire generation in the East lost because they were on the wrong side. West Germany has an obligation to see eastern Germany through the difficult times of reunification and the healing that must happen. It took generations for East German lives to be crushed. It will take generations for Germany to feel whole again.

Chapter Eighteen

The Wall Comes Down—1989

Martin visited East Germany again in the summer of 1989. He came back to Canada saying he felt a growing restlessness there. He had no idea that only three months later, on November 9, the Wall would come down, thanks to the efforts of the German people. Americans like to claim President Reagan brought the Wall down, but it was not the politicians—it was a Lutheran minister in Leipzig who rallied the people every Monday night in a silent, candlelit protest. Eventually the crowds grew too big and the commander of the East German police advised the Russian commander that next Monday "we will shoot to disburse the crowd." The Russian commander declined any help. It was at this moment that the East German regime imploded. Suddenly, the East German army abandoned their posts and watched as a torrent of people flowed across the border to the West, celebrating their victory over Communism.

A few weeks later the West German government sent truck loads of West German army uniforms to the garrisons in East Germany with the order for the solders to wear them. For 40 years the armies had watched each other across the iron curtain with binoculars, loaded guns ready. Now, with the new uniforms, the East German army saw no reason to continue this absurdity; the soldiers on the other side looked the same! History will show the Wall coming down was both a happy AND bloodless event.

Our family returned again in 1990. How different it was! No Checkpoint Charlie or guards, and the Wall had almost disappeared. We went to Berlin to celebrate the anniversary of the fall of the Wall. It was fantastic listening to an orchestra playing Beethoven's Ninth Symphony near the Brandenburg Gate. Of course, East Berlin still looked drab and desolate in contrast to the garishness of West Berlin with its prosperous shops, clubs, and theatres. Tessa preferred East Berlin at that time, and was almost nostalgic for the way it had been. In 1990 she returned to Prague, Czechoslovakia with a group of 500 Canadian teachers to teach English at Charles University. The Czechs had just gone through their "Velvet Revolution" when they too overthrew Communism.

We have returned to Germany almost every year since 1990 with grandchildren in tow. Our last visit was in the summer of 2004. The united Germany of today still is not well-off or truly united. The unemployment rate is 12% in Western Germany and 25% in Eastern Germany, and there is a general dissatisfaction with the current situation. The population in Eastern Germany is mostly elderly because young people have left for Western Germany hoping to find jobs. It's rare to see children in the former East Germany, and schools have closed because there is no population to support them. For example, in the small town of Geising near Martin's village, population 3,000, they usually have an enrollment in the first grade of 20–25 children. In 2004, only one six-year-old child registered. Some are nostalgic for the former East Germany when the State looked after them from the cradle to the grave. In the West, they grumble that reunification has cost too much and they see their benefits and pensions slowly disappearing. The government simply cannot afford the generous handouts of the past.

In Eastern Germany, we were impressed with the number of cars on the road and freshly painted houses, but there are still many abandoned farms and properties left by owners seeking a better life elsewhere. Our West German friends seem to know little about East Germany's past under Communism or the allied bombing of Dresden. When asked why, one friend said, "I was born in 1952, shortly after the end of the war, and nobody wanted to talk about the war then. I think Germans wanted to blot out their painful past because they were still dealing with the consequences. After all, most German cities had been destroyed by allied bombing with a heavy loss of life. So we had our own worries and knew very little about the Communist era in East Germany unless we had family there."

4000 acres of the historic city of DRESDEN destroyed within 16 hours by planned massive area firebombing which consumed the oxygen. Pyres on the Altmarkt burned for months to dispose of the bodies.

Reconciliation

The fire-bombing of Dresden, just three months before the end of the war, caused a firestorm that left one of Europe's most Baroque cities in ruins. So many were killed that piles of charred bodies had to be burned in public squares rather than buried. A total of

WW II destruction of German Cities showing % in black.

635,000 civilians were killed in Allied bombing raids devastating most of Germany's cities. In 1940, Coventry was subjected to the single most concentrated attack on a British city in World War II. The raid lasted 11 hours, 4,000 homes were damaged or destroyed, as well as the great medieval church of St. Michaels—the only cathedral to be destroyed in Britain. The official death toll of 554 was far less than Dresden's. The day after the blitz, Coventry decided to rebuild the cathedral as a testament to peace and reconciliation.

In 1951 at the age of 21, Martin emigrated to Canada with a strong desire to leave the rubble and continuous wars of Europe behind and start a new life. He visited England in the early 1970s and went to Coventry. In the ruins of the Cathedral, he found a stone plaque with an inscription saying that Coventry and Dresden were twin cities. In 1956, the ancient English city of Coventry had twinned with Dresden. In an effort to end the destruction of war, the citizens of both cities had risen above the rubble and extended their hands in friendship and remembrance, pledging that such destruction shall never happen again. Martin was moved to tears standing in front of the plaque. There was hope after all!

On June 22, 2004, a British-built cross was hoisted onto Dresden's Frauenkirche cathedral as part of its reconstruction. This gesture of reconciliation coincided with new controversy about whether the 1945 allied bombing of the city was justified. The giant golden cross was built by Alan Smith, the son of a British bomber pilot who took part in the World War II raid, killing 100,000 people or more and destroyed 80 percent of the city. British supporters of the reconstruction, due to be completed in 2005, see the cross as another symbol of reconciliation. Weeks before, Chancellor Gerhard

Schroeder became the first German leader to attend
D-Day memorial ceremonies.

Support from around the world came to Dresden
to fund the reconstruction of the Frauenkirche. The
Dean of Coventry Cathedral heads an international
group which supplies information to people around the
world who are being misled by nationalistic or religious
propaganda. These people mainly young and impres-
sionable and have no way of knowing whether what
they are being told is true because they have little contact with the outside world. The boy soldiers of Africa
and the young suicide bombers of the Muslim world are
cases in point.

Coincidentally, Martin was attending a 60 year
class reunion in his hometown of Altenberg, 35 kilometers south of Dresden. As he was driving back to the
city, he turned on his car radio and heard about the ceremony at the *Frauenkirche*. Remembering the night the
magnificent cathedral, built in the 18th century, suc-
cumbed to the firestorm, he decided to attend the ceremony. He stood in the large, silent crowd and listened
as the Duke of Kent spoke about the wrongs of the past
and the hopes of the future. The Duke, who heads a
foundation helping to rebuild the church, said in fluent
German, "This is a wonderful project that unites people
who were once enemies in a strong and lasting friendship." The magnificent *Ode to Joy*, sung with such emo-
tion by the choir, brought tears to people's eyes, some
of whom had survived that dreadful February night.
Martin watched as the cupola rose from the ground

amid applause, until it came to rest far up on top of the sandstone tower which was pockmarked with some of the old, charred stones. Good will of mankind had triumphed over hate and destruction. For Martin it was finally closure to the most painful period of his life.

Epilogue

As I watched the 60th anniversary D-Day ceremonies on June 6, 2004, I wept. I wept for my father who never grew old, for the loved ones who never returned home, and for the futility of war. My father's brother Charles wrote a book of poetry after the war called Memento and paid a tribute to my father in his poem:

Our Jack went down to the sea,
As Jack Tars do,
And some men find they must,
Gay, jolly souls throw fetters free,
And sail the oceans wide and blue,
Both bold they are and dauntless too,
They bring the commerce of the World,
And lay it at our feet.

I see him joyously setting sail,
With gallant and spinnaker blown,
I see him bucking the blinding gale,
I see him courting a dusky "frail,"
O'er horizons far and wide,
I see him blistering in tropic calm,
I hear him cuss and rant,
I hear his laughter above the gale
As he trims again his tattered sail.

I see him coming home again,
His face all burnished gold,
The roll of the sea still in his gait,
A brilliant macaw set on his pate,
His arms abrim with treasures rare,
And joy and laughter's in the air,
It's great to have him home.

Once again he sets his billowing sail,
But now sneaks off with the dawn,
In the hell of war he carries on,
The joy and laughter are not gone,
But stilled beneath the grim and tragic task,
To bring her home again at last, at last.

I see him now where he is gone,
To the calm of the depths below,
Where the turmoil and strife of mortal life,
Are scorned with a loud "Yo Ho!"
These sailor men who are lost at sea,

Make the port of eternal peace.
Landlubbers are apt to think them dead,
But me, I like to think,
Old Father Neptune gathers his men,
In merry company.
With the treasure rare of the fabulous seas,
More wealth than in all the World,
Lying at their feet.

His soul is enshrined in the Heaven above,
His memory is cherished on Earth,
And oft when I stand by the sea at night,
I hear his laughter above the gale,
As he trims against his phantom sail.

I sometimes wonder if the ultimate sacrifice he made was worth it, but every year I remember him with tears in my eyes on November 11 (Remembrance Day). The Merchant Navy has a war memorial for those who perished in World War II in a small park across from the Tower of London. His ship was Empire Endurance, and his name, Jack Osbourne Durling, is listed there under the name of his ship. He was awarded three medals.

Martin's Final Thoughts

Martin often tells the following story.

We had 4 children aged 6–12 years who were in our country house 40 km away in the Laurentians with a sitter, when Tessa and I were invited by friends to a party in Montreal. It was bitterly cold and windy, with snow blowing across the highway. The wind chill must have been 40 below. At 2 a.m., we drove from Montreal up the Auto route to the mountains. Our car was a temperamental Mercedes. Suddenly the car stopped—we later found out it was a faulty fuel pump. We pulled over and waited. There was no traffic either way. I told Tessa this is serious. We were not properly dressed, and the cold would penetrate the car and freeze us within a few hours. We huddled together, waiting. About half an hour later, a car stopped. It was a French Canadian schoolteacher from St. Jerome. He said, "You cannot stay here, come quickly into my car!" He then drove us 15 minutes to his house, woke up his wife who made us hot chocolate, called a tow truck, brought us back to our stalled car, made sure we were stowed away in the warm cabin of the tow truck, and said goodbye. Before he left, I told him that he had probably saved our lives and was there anything I could do for him in return. "No, no," he said. I insisted, saying "I want to thank you; can I give you

*$100?" (a lot of money then). "No, no," he said, "JUST
PASS IT ON." I never met this kind man again, but I have
PASSED IT ON many times, and I have told the story
many times. Good things have happened to you too—
try to PASS THEM ON!*

It is now the beginning of March, 2002. Renate
Nickels and her daughter Claudia are with us in Costa
Rica for a visit. Renate's husband and Claudia's father
was Peter Nickels, my best friend for 50 years. We met
in Montreal in 1952; just after we both arrived there
from Germany. Peter died in 2001 after a battle with
cancer, and having them both here now brings back a
lot of memories and thoughts about life, death, and
dying. In February, a few days before Peter passed on,
we spoke on the telephone and then I wrote to him the
following letter:

Dear Peter,

It was good to hear your voice and our spirits bonded, even if only for a few
minutes. My thoughts are with you and your family.

As you know, I have been interested in spiritual matters for
some time and particularly so after my triple by-pass in 1993. I have read
dozens of books on the subject of reincarnation and the consensus seems
to be the following: Our spirit or soul has lived in many other bodies before
ours. It lives in our body to go through life experiences in order to mature.
When our earth time ends, the spirit moves to a celestial place to join
other spirits. Many books describe this transition as a happy event. As
the spirit leaves the body, a great peace comes over it. There are descrip-
tions of a tunnel with a lot of light at the end and a feeling of incredible
well-being and happiness as the spirit passes through the tunnel into a
very bright light. Spirits of friends or relatives who have made the journey
before are there to help the transition and to welcome your spirit into this
new world. Time and distance do not exist there, it is universal.

The ones you leave behind should not be sad. You did what you came to do. Their spirit and yours will always be connected. When their time comes for the same journey, your spirit will be there and you will be together again. In time, your spirit will be living in another body and so the spiritual life continues. This is a very condensed picture of what some religions say and philosophers back to Plato have talked about. I believe it is so.

So, here is the deal! When you get to the other side, have a good look around and get your bearings. Then when I come, and I won't be far behind, we can go on new adventures in true Max and Moritz style. Simply because what we had here was too good not to continue! And please remember to send me a message about what this new world is like. I will tune in my receivers.

So with a big long hug to you and everyone in your family my very best wishes go to you on this journey. With all my love to you and your family, your old friend,

Eberhart

Postscript:

After Peter's funeral, friends and family gathered at a reception. Our daughter Megan represented us, as we were in Costa Rica. A lady walked up to Megan and asked, "Are you Martin Borner's daughter?" When Megan said yes she continued, "I am a medium and I have a message from Peter for your father. He wants to tell Martin that he is fine and that everything is as they both had imagined it to be!"

Generations before us have come and gone. Our time will come too for the journey to the other side of which we know little only that it is there. While we are here on earth and living, it is our obligation to do our best for others, our family, and ourselves. Looking back now, that is what I have done. When the time comes to check out of this life, I will be ready to go on the journey. My family and friends shall have no regrets nor be sorry for me or sad. Before long, I will be together again with them as I expect to be together with my son, parents, and family who have taken the journey before me. I have had a good life, full of happiness and also tragedies.

I have always tried to listen to my inner voice to give me guidance. Without it I would not have lived long on this earth. Who was it that helped me along? Was it my guardian angel? I will find out when I am in the other dimension. For those who are reading this, take heart. Follow your dreams, do unto others as you would want them to do unto you, and listen to your inner voice!

And in conclusion,
as my departed friend Peter would say,

CIAO!